12th SS PANZER DIVISION HITLERJUGEND

CASEMATE | ILLUSTRATED

Auch Du

◯ CASEMATE | ILLUSTRATED

12th SS PANZER DIVISION HITLERJUGEND

FROM FORMATION TO THE BATTLE OF CAEN

MASSIMILIANO AFIERO

CASEMATE | ILLUSTRATED

CIS0027

Print Edition: ISBN 978-1-63624-168-5
Digital Edition: ISBN 978-1-63624-169-2

Translated and adapted from *12.SS-Panzer-Division Hitlerjugend* © Associazione Cultural Ritterkreuz, 2020.
English-language edition © 2022 Casemate Publishers
Translator: Ralph Riccio
Artwork by Paul Hewitt

Design by Battlefield Design
Printed and bound in Turkey by Megaprint

CASEMATE PUBLISHERS (US)
Telephone (610) 853-9131
Fax (610) 853-9146
Email: casemate@casematepublishers.com
www.casematepublishers.com

CASEMATE PUBLISHERS (UK)
Telephone (01865) 241249
Email: casemate-uk@casematepublishers.co.uk
www.casematepublishers.co.uk

All photos contained in this book are derived from archival sources, including the US National Archives and Records Administration, Library of Congress, Bundesarchiv, and the US Military History Institute, unless otherwise noted.

Half-title page image: Hitlerjugend divisional insignia.
Page 2 image: Hitlerjugend recruitment poster by Ottomar Anton.
Title page image: A self-propelled Wespe of I./SS-Pz.Art.Rgt.12.
Contents page map: Objective Caen, June/July 1944.
Contents page image: Nazi Party rally, Nuremberg, 1938.

This study was made possible thanks to the collaboration of many friends and colleagues, who shared with me their research concerning the 12th SS Panzer Division: in particular, Cesare Veronesi of Bologna, Stefano Canavassi of Livorno, and Lorenzo Silvestri of Trieste. Thanks also to all the other friends and collectors in the Association for providing unpublished iconographic and documentary material from their private collections and archives.

Images are credited as follows: Bundesarchiv, Germany (BA); Berlin Document Center (BDC); Washington, D.C. National Archives and Records Administration (NARA); Ukrainian Central State Archives; Institute of Modern History of Ljubljana (MNZS); Charles Trang personal collection; Herbert Walther personal collection; Hubert Meyer personal collection; Günther Scappini personal collection.

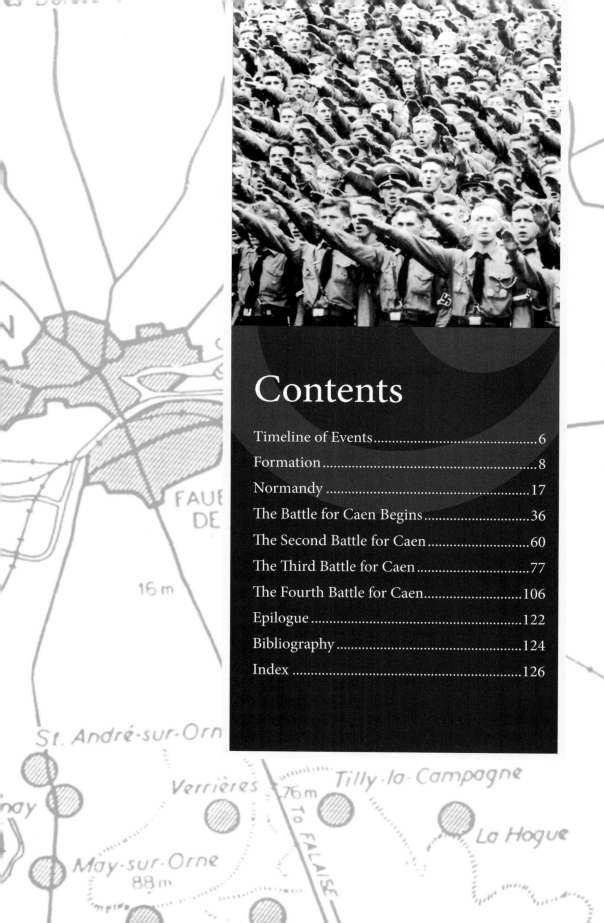

Contents

Timeline of Events

Created in 1943, primarily as an emergency response force in France to repel the expected Allied invasion from the sea, the SS-Hitlerjugend division performed its duties with extreme valor and determination, blocking the enemy advance and thwarting Allied plans on more than one occasion. Following the June 6, 1944 Allied landings in Normandy, a bridgehead was established within a day. However, six weeks later the panzer divisions, notably the Hitlerjugend, had not been subdued and the city of Caen stood firm.

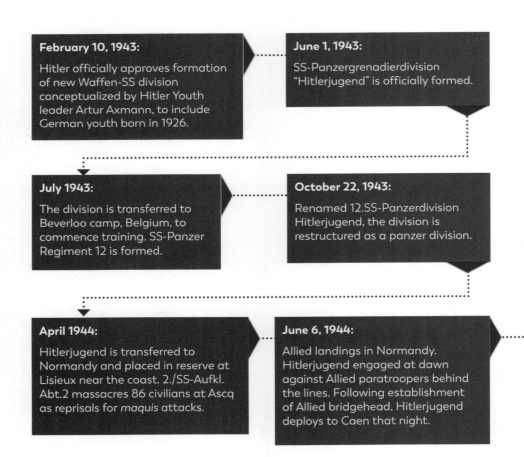

February 10, 1943:

Hitler officially approves formation of new Waffen-SS division conceptualized by Hitler Youth leader Artur Axmann, to include German youth born in 1926.

June 1, 1943:

SS-Panzergrenadierdivision "Hitlerjugend" is officially formed.

July 1943:

The division is transferred to Beverloo camp, Belgium, to commence training. SS-Panzer Regiment 12 is formed.

October 22, 1943:

Renamed 12.SS-Panzerdivision Hitlerjugend, the division is restructured as a panzer division.

April 1944:

Hitlerjugend is transferred to Normandy and placed in reserve at Lisieux near the coast. 2./SS-Aufkl. Abt.2 massacres 86 civilians at Ascq as reprisals for *maquis* attacks.

June 6, 1944:

Allied landings in Normandy. Hitlerjugend engaged at dawn against Allied paratroopers behind the lines. Following establishment of Allied bridgehead, Hitlerjugend deploys to Caen that night.

A young 12th SS grenadier wearing an M44 camouflage uniform.

June 7, 1944:

First battle for Caen commences.

June 11, 1944:

Second battle for Caen commences.

June 13, 1944:

Battle of Villers-Bocage: Wittman's Tigers wreak havoc on Allied armor.

June 25, 1944:

Third battle for Caen (first battle of the Odon) opens, followed by the British Operation *Epsom* the next day.

July 1, 1944:

Fourth battle for Caen begins with British Operation *Windsor* threatening Carpiquet airfield.

| Formation

After the disastrous defeat of Stalingrad in February 1943, Adolf Hitler mobilized all available resources to finally destroy Soviet Russia, with the concept of *Total-Krieg*, total war. The formation of an SS-Hitlerjugend division was part of this great project.

The original idea belonged to Artur Axmann, head of the Hitler Youth, and SS-Gruppenführer Gottlob Berger, head of the SS-Hauptamt (the Central Office of the SS) and responsible for Waffen-SS enlistment. The plan was to create a new division of the Waffen-SS, composed exclusively of volunteers from the Hitlerjugend, the organization that included all the German youth born in the year 1926. On February 10, 1943, Hitler officially approved the formation of the new division.

Artur Axmann with German youths. (NARA)

Divisional Order of Battle, July 1943

Kommando, SS-Panzer-Grenadier-Division

SS-Pz.Gren.Rgt.1 Hitlerjugend

    I.-III.Bataillon

SS-Pz.Gren.Rgt.2 Hitlerjugend

    I.-III.Bataillon

SS-Panzer-Regiment Hitlerjugend

SS-Artillerie-Rgt.(mot.) Hitlerjugend

SS-Kradschützen-Regiment Hitlerjugend

    I.-II.Bataillon

SS-Panzer-Jäger-Abteilung

SS-Flak-Abt.(mot.)

SS-Pionier-Btl.(mot.)

SS-Nachrichten-Abteilung (mot.)

SS-Pz.Gren.Ausbildungs und Ersatz-Btl.

SS-Div.Nachschub-Truppen

SS-Verwaltungs-Truppen

SS-Kraftfahrpark-Truppen

SS-Sanitäts-Truppen

Some 840 officers and 4,000 non-commissioned officers were needed, some of whom had to come from the other formations of the Waffen-SS and from Heer units. Axmann estimated that he could supply at least 30,000 youths; however, recruitment did not live up to expectations.

The division was officially created on June 1, 1943. On the 24th, an order from the SS-FHA (SS-Führungshauptamt, the operational headquarters of the SS) established the final operational details for the division. The new unit was named SS-Panzergrenadierdivision "Hitlerjugend."

Transfer to Belgium

In July 1943, the division was sent to the Beverloo camp, 72 kilometers southeast of Antwerp, in Belgium. Recruitment was still insufficient and some 50 Heer officers were transferred in. "Pre-military education" was handled exclusively by Hitlerjugend leaders, all of whom were war veterans wounded while serving at the front. A former head of the Hitlerjugend and a Waffen-SS officer, Herbert Taege, wrote: "the training program of the pre-military camps was restricted to 160 hours. It included small arms firing, maneuver training, etc. At the end of this training the boys received the 'war training certificate,' but it had nothing to do with the actual basic military education of the armed forces."

Considering that most of the young volunteers, including many combat veterans, were in poor physical condition, Divisional Adjutant, SS-Stubaf. Heinrich Springer, set physical fitness as a priority in the training and only after that came military training proper.

SS-Stubaf. Heinrich Springer.
(BDC)

9

Fritz Witt during the Balkans campaign, with war correspondent Gunther d'Alquen. (NARA)

Training with antitank guns at the Beverloo camp. (NARA)

Very young members of the Hitlerjugend visiting the division while in training.

Training was haphazard due to a lack of equipment. As of October 1, 1943, the division had only 7,540 rifles out of the 15,751 needed. The situation was even more critical for machine guns (431 out of 1,584), tanks (3 out of 198), armored infantry vehicles and armored cars (none out of 347) and non-armored vehicles (12 out of 3,219).

In October, it was decided to reorganize the division, not as a formation of armored grenadiers, but as a panzer division to be incorporated into I.SS-Panzerkorps. On October 22, 1943, the division was renamed 12.SS-Panzerdivision Hitlerjugend. The unit was organized following the structure of a 1943 panzer division, with two regiments of armored grenadiers, one armored regiment, one regiment of artillery with four groups (one of which was equipped with self-propelled guns), a tank destroyer group, an antiaircraft unit, a pioneer unit, a signals unit, and the other service units.

The first batches of recruits, including Flemish volunteers, were absorbed by the Panzergrenadier regiments, SS-Pz.Gr.Rgt.25 and SS-Pz.Gr.Rgt.26, the latter transferred to Maria-Ter-Heide, 15 kilometers northeast of Antwerp. An artillery regiment was quartered near the Beverloo camp, in the Mol area. A reconnaissance battalion and the medical detachment, commanded by SS-Stubaf. Rolf Schulz, were based at Turnhout, 48 kilometers northeast of Antwerp. A pioneer battalion took up positions at Herentals on the Albert Canal, the logistics services in Geel, and a panzer regiment at the Mailly-le-Camp training area, 35 kilometers south of Chalons-sur-Marne. Divisional HQ was located at Zwanestrand near Turnhout. SS-Pz.Gren.A.-u.E.-Btl. "HJ," the reinforcement and training battalion, was headquartered at Arnhem in the Netherlands.

Swearing-in ceremony of SS-Pz.Gr.Rgt.25 recruits, in the presence of Kurt Meyer, in the background, November 1943. (NARA)

Training continued apace with recruits occasionally engaged in sweep operations in Belgium and the Netherlands to flush out partisans. After the fitness regime and individual training, collective training was given in squads, platoons, and companies, with a view to soonest combat-readiness. This phase was completed on December 5–7 to coincide with a visit from Axmann, who was highly impressed with his "lads."

In January 1944, the situation improved with the arrival of vehicles from the Italian army. But the lack of fuel remained critical and impaired training significantly. However, individual training was excellent. In February, when the first divisional exercises began, the HJ fielded more than 20,000 troops, whose average age, including officers and NCOs, was 18. Their morale was extraordinarily high, confirmed during their later deployment in Normandy. Equipment finally began arriving and in larger quantities; for example, SS-Pz. Rgt.12 had 97 PzKpfw.IVs and eight PzKpfw.V Panthers.

Formation of the Panzer Regiment

Panzer Abteilung personnel came from the I.Pz.Abteilung Leibstandarte (LSAAH), detached from the division at the beginning of April 1943 after the battle of Kharkov. In mid-June, SS-Ogruf. Sepp Dietrich placed SS-Sturmbannführer Max Wünsche, hitherto commander of the I./SS-Pz.Rgt.1, in command of the new SS-Panzer-Regiment, the unit now based at Mailly-le-Camp, France.

5.Kompanie, II.SS-Pz.Rgt.12 crews lined up in front of their "new" PzKpfw IVs Ausf H for inspection. The vehicles are painted in dark yellow with a green and brown camouflage pattern. All crewmembers wear leather jackets and trousers from the Italian Navy. (Michael Cremin collection)

In Profile:
SS-Oberführer Fritz Witt

Witt commanded the Hitlerjugend from June 24, 1943 to June 14, 1944. He was born in Hagen-Hohenlimburg, in 1908, into a merchant family. Having lost his job in 1931, he joined the Nazi Party, serving with what evolved into the SS-Sonderkommando Berlin. In January 1935, he took command of SS-Standarte Deutschland—which later became Das Reich—in which he participated in the 1939 invasion of Poland. As CO SS-Regiment Deutschland, he took part in the invasion of the Low Countries and the battle for France. In October 1940, he assumed command of an LSSAH battalion in the invasion of Greece and took part in the battle of Kleisoura Pass against the British (his brother Franz was killed in the action). He took command of the embryonic Hitlerjugend in June 1943 before the division was transferred to the Normandy front. Serving with distinction during the Normandy campaign, his tenure was benighted by the SS massacre of 86 French civilians at Ascq and the murder of

SS-Brigdf. Fritz Witt. (BDC)

Canadian PoWs in the Ardenne Abbey massacre. Witt was killed in a Royal Navy bombardment on June 14, 1944 in his Venoix command post. He held the Iron Cross (1st and 2nd Class), the German Cross in Gold, and the Knight's Cross of the Iron Cross with Oak Leaves.

SS-Staf. Witt during the Kharkov counteroffensive in March 1943, giving orders to one of his soldiers. (US NARA)

SS-Ostuf. Rudolf von Ribbentrop. (BDC)

The actual formation of SS-Panzer Regiment 12 did not begin until the end of July, when the nucleus of personnel available, a final force of 71 officers, 850 non-commissioned officers (NCOs) and 1,380 men, was attained.

Wünsche hoped that the new division would be equipped with the latest panzer models, but instead of the Tiger tanks, only "old" Panthers and even older PzKpfw IVs arrived. The tank crews also received Kriegsmarine *U-Boote* uniforms, material originally from the Italian Navy seized by the Germans after September 8, 1943.

The situation improved progressively with the arrival of further Panzer IVs. As of January 1, 1944, 38 Panzer IVs were operational. Also in January, the unit was transferred to Hasselt, near Beverloo camp. Training continued with difficulty due to a lack of practice ammunition and fuel. On February 5, SS-Panzer-Regiment 12 reported 79 Panzer IVs and seven Panthers operational, with 18 Panzer IVs and one Panther under repair.

The following day the regiment conducted a field exercise in the presence of Generaloberst Guderian, General Geyr von Schweppenburg, and SS-Ogruf. Dietrich. The future delivery of more panzers depended heavily on the outcome of the exercise itself. Despite the excellent performance, the division continued to suffer a severe shortage of weapons, materials, vehicles, and fuel.

Following the departure of the Frundsberg and Hohenstaufen divisions for the Galician front in early April, Hitlerjugend was ordered to Normandy. It was headquartered in the Louviers region, with Wünsche's command post (CP) in Acquigny.

On April 12, the Panzerflak-Zug, equipped with 12 Flakpanzer 38 (t) armed with 2cm Flak 38 pieces, arrived from its training in Germany. On April 20, SS-Stubaf. Jürgensen of I./SS-Panzer-Regiment 12 reported 26 Panthers on issue.

Wünsche, who was part of the I./SS-Pz.Korps delegation sent on an official visit to Hitler's headquarters on the occasion of his birthday (April 20), took the opportunity to show the Führer photos of the anti-aircraft defense tank, devised by the Hitlerjugend which had mounted a 2cm Flakvierling on the chassis of a Panzer IV. This prototype served as the basis for the development of the Flakpanzer IV Wirbelwind.

As of April 30, SS-Panzer-Regiment 12 mustered six Panzer IIs, one Panzer IV L/24 (short gun), three Panzer IV L/43s (long gun), 90 Panzer IV L/48s, 26 Panthers, and three Flakpanzer IVs with 2cm Flakvierling.

In May, Hitlerjugend had to cede 2,042 men, including 13 officers, to 1.SS-Panzer-Division LSSAH undergoing reorganization in Belgium. On May 21, eight Panthers arrived followed by another convoy with another eight, two days later. On May 31, two new convoys each transported seven Panzer Vs to Louviers station.

On June 1, 1944, the Hitlerjugend was considered operational. The panzer regiment now fielded 91 Panzer IVs and 48 operational Panthers, with nine panzers under repair. Fortuitously, 30 more Panthers arrived a week before the Allied landings of June 6.

PzKpfw IVs of 6./SS-Pz.Rgt.12 during a halt in a Flemish village on an exercise. (NARA)

Normandy

On November 3, 1943, Führer directive number 51 ordered the strengthening of defenses in northern France in view of the imminent Allied invasion from the sea, scheduled for the spring of 1944. This also included the stepped-up supply of weapons and equipment for the new Hitlerjugend division.

SS-Obstgruf. Paul Hausser. (BDC)

In April 1944, the division transferred to the Normandy front. The threat of encirclement of 1.Panzerarmee in the southern sector of the Eastern Front, between the Bug and the Dnieper, forced the OKW to transfer the II.SS-Panzerkorps, including the two new *Panzerdivisionen*, SS Hohenstaufen and Frundsberg, to the Eastern Front. Hitlerjugend took over the Frundsberg billets, between the lower Seine and the Orne. The division's chief of staff, SS-Stubaf. Hubert Meyer, was surprised to learn that the division had been located so close to the coast, at Lisieux, in contrast to the directive that officially placed Hitlerjugend in reserve.

Meyer then met General Geyr von Schweppenburg in Paris to find out where the division was to be stationed. As a result, the division was assigned to an area farther south, between the towns of Nogent-le-Roi, Houdan, Pacy-sur-Eure, Louriers, Elbeuf, Bernay, Vimoutiers, Sees, and Mortagne. The Panzer-Regiment was assigned the northeastern sector (Elbeuf, Louviers) to be closer to the crossings over the Seine: Schweppenburg, Supreme Commander of the Western Front and Heeresgruppe B, believed that the Allied landing would take place north of the Seine.

Erwin Rommel. (BDC)

An SdKfz 232 of SS-Pz.Aufkl.Abt.12. (Hubert Meyer collection)

Hitlerjugend PzKpfw IV "625" on the move. (NARA)

Leo Geyr von Schweppenburg. (BDC)

SS-Pionier Bataillon 12 was located on both banks of the Eure River from Pacy to Autreuil, while the Flak Abteilung took up positions near the Dreux airport. SS-Pz.Gr.Rgt.26 was transferred to Houdan, in order to work together with its battalion of armored grenadiers on halftracks (III./26) with the Panzer-Regiment. SS-Pz.Gr.Rgt.25 was assigned the western part of the area (Bernay, Orbec, Vimoutiers, Sees) for a possible engagement to the west. The artillery regiment was positioned in the center of the area, near Damville, the reconnaissance battalion around Rugles, and the signals detachment at Verneuil and Brézolles. The SS-Panzerjäger Abteilung was headquartered near Nogent-Le-Roi, while the Werfer Abteilung was moved to the area between Dreux and Nonancourt. The service units were relocated to Mortagne to the south and the divisional staff at Acon, 7 kilometers west of Nonancourt.

A large-caliber gun of the Atlantic Wall defenses.

A motorized Hitlerjugend column on the march, spring 1944.

Sabotage and Reprisals

During the night of April 1/2, 1944, as Hitlerjugend troops were transferring by train from Belgium to Normandy, the lines were sabotaged by the *maquis*. Trains were held up either side of the town of Ascq. Although the Hitlerjugend sustained no casualties, daybreak would see the appearance of Allied fighter-bombers (*Jabos*) that would place the Germans in grave danger.

While waiting for the railway engineers to repair the damage, SS-Ostuf. Walter Hauck commander of 2./SS-Aufkl.Abt.2, on his own initiative searched the village and rounded up all men between 17 and 50, acting on his belief that they were sheltering the perpetrators. No information was forthcoming so Hauck ordered them to be shot in small groups, to force the *maquis* to surrender. The French gendarmerie at Lannoy, warned of the incident, did not intervene and the small Heer detachment in Ascq, unable to intervene and communicate by telephone, sent a runner to the German headquarters at Lille. At 0115 on April 2, when 86 people had already been slaughtered, the massacre was stopped by the courageous intervention of Leutnant Fricke, sent to the scene with a unit of the Feldgendarmerie, after a heated quarrel between the two officers.

Organization of Defenses

While the troops were waiting to learn their final destination, the divisional commander, SS-Brigdf. Fritz Witt, and Meyer himself, reconnoitered the terrain to prepare defensive measures along the coast in the sector at the mouth of the Seine, at Bayeux.

General der Artillerie Erich Marks of LXXXIV.Armeekorps at Saint-Lô briefed them on the situation in his sector that stretched from just east of the mouth of the River Orne along the Normandy coast, to the River Vire, and east, north, and west, along the coast of the Cotentin Peninsula to Avranches. Marcks considered two possibilities for the upcoming

Allied landing: a landing between the Orne and the Vire and on the east coast of the Cotentin Peninsula, with Paris as the main target or massive landings either side of the Cotentin Peninsula to capture the port of Cherbourg.

Already in position were the 716. and 352.Inf.Div., between Merville and the mouth of the Vire. The former was a so-called "static" division, without transport, but above all with a serious troop shortfall. The 77.Inf.Div was located around Caen as a reserve but was relieved at the end of April by the 21.Pz.Div.

The greatest effort in the construction of the defensive installations had been concentrated in the northern part of the east coast of the Cotentin Peninsula and toward the port of Cherbourg. The strengthening of the positions in the sector between Merville and the estuary of the Vire was only begun much later. Artillery bunkers were still under construction as were obstacles against airborne troops and landing troops. Marcks expected the first Allied landing to be successful: he was unsure of being able to repel the enemy with the forces available to him and hoped that Hitlerjugend would be assigned to him. Witt and Meyer were very impressed by Marcks, a veteran of the Eastern Front, from which he had returned missing a leg. His assessment of the situation was clear and convincing. Witt and Meyer then went on a reconnaissance along the coast. Here, they discovered that the 716. Inf.Div. position consisted of a line of defenses along the beach, 800 to 1,200 meters apart. Behind these were a few antitank positions and the division's artillery deployed completely in the open. Furthermore, French civilians were noticed moving freely between positions, without any precautions or safeguards.

Elements of SS-Pz.Aufkl.Abt.12 moving through a village. (Hubert Meyer collection)

In the meantime, Schweppenburg issued a directive to the Hitlerjugend in which the preparation of three action plans in the event of an Allied landing was ordered: 1) Crossing of the Seine between Paris and Rouen for action between the Somme and the Seine; 2) Deployment for action between the mouths of the Seine and the Orne; 3) Deployment for action in the area northwest and west of Caen.

After inspecting the roads and bridges, the divisional staff prepared the plans for the three different actions, codenamed A, B, and C. To deploy the units in width and depth, four directions of travel were planned. One of the four routes was to be used by tracked vehicles, for example those of the Panzer-Regiment, the SS-Schützenpanzer Bataillon (III./26), and I. Artillerie-Abteilung (self-propelled guns). Armored grenadier regiments 25 and 26 (without their third battalions), each with an attached artillery detachment, and the other units of the division had to march on the other three routes, all this to avoid traffic jams on the roads.

During May, specialist training was intensified but due to Allied air activity, had to take place in the evening with continued focus on intercepting and eliminating enemy airborne forces. The vehicles and the panzers were always well camouflaged from Allied aerial reconnaissance.

The Flak-Abteilung, the anti-aircraft unit, moved from Dreux in mid-May, along the Seine to protect the bridges. The 1st and 3rd Batteries, equipped with 8.8cm Flak pieces, took up positions in Elbeuf, the 2nd (8.8cm pieces) and 4th (3.7cm pieces) took up positions first at

A Hitlerjugend Flak gun during training, spring 1944. (NARA)

A Hitlerjugend 2cm Flakvierling in Normandy. (MNZS)

SS-Hstuf. Hans Siegel. (BDC)

Pont-de-l'Arche and then around Gaillon. The 14.(Flak).Kompanie of SS-Pz.Gr.Rgt.26, subordinated to the Flak-Abteilung, also took up a position in Gaillon and shot down an estimated five enemy bombers but failed to prevent the destruction of the bridges.

The Panzer Abteilung still lacked command and recovery tanks and the Werfer Abteilung lacked tow tractors. In practice, both *Abteilungen* were not yet ready for action and could not even train. In the artillery regiment, there were no ammunition vehicles and the reconnaissance battalion lacked armored cars, essential for their reconnaissance missions. Despite the lack of all of this equipment, the division was considered ready for action on June 1, 1944. The general command of I.SS-Panzerkorps reported: "the division, with the exception of the Werfer Abteilung and the Panzer Abteilung, is completely ready for any action on the western front."

Although Hitler did not believe much in the hypothesis of an imminent Allied landing on the coasts of northern France, Hitlerjugend for its part continued to prepare. In the Panzer-Regiment, for example, crews were on constant alert as witnessed by the CO 8.Pz.Kompanie, Hans Siegel:

> Squadrons of enemy bombers fly above us every night and we are expecting the launch of paratroopers at any moment. Max Wünsche prepared for this eventuality by ordering absolute silence and ordering us to stay hidden during the day. The village where we were quartered offered a peaceful appearance and the soldiers slept, armed. During the night, everyone was awake. The crews were ready for action near their vehicles and the ammunition was ready to be loaded on board. This state of alert began four weeks before the invasion.

SS-Ostuf. Wilhelm Beck. (BDC)

SS-Untersturmführer Willy Kändler, assigned by the Panzer-Regiment to the divisional staff as liaison officer, wrote: "on the afternoon of June 4 ... the division sent me an urgent order, about the immediate cessation of the exercises since the Allied invasion was imminent."

Allied Plans

Allied strategists had begun drawing up plans for the invasion of France as early as May 1943, planning to use the shortest route, via the Pas de Calais. But precisely at that point, the Atlantic Wall was more solid and 15.Armee with its 17 divisions was located in that sector. So Normandy was then chosen as the new landing point, defended by 7.Armee with its 11 divisions, making the Germans believe, however, that the real landing point was always the Pas de Calais. While the Allied air forces began to systematically bomb the entire railway and road system of northern France, the task of drawing up the battle development plan was entrusted to General Montgomery, as commander of the land forces: the British forces would land in eastern Normandy and the Americans in western Normandy.

Divisional Order of Battle, June 1, 1944

Kommando, SS-Panzer-Division
    Stab der Division
    SS-Divisions Kartenstelle (mot.)
SS-Feldendarmerie-Kompanie (mot.) 12
SS-Division-Begleit-Kompanie (mot.)
SS-Panzer-Grenadier-Regiment 25
    I.-III.SS.Inf.Btl (mot.)
    13.Inf.Geschütz-Kompanie
    14.le.Flak.Kp.(Sf)
    15.Aufkl.-Kompanie (mot.)
    16.Pionier-Kompanie
SS-Panzer-Grenadier-Regiment 26
    I.-II.SS-Inf.Btl (mot.)
    III.SS-Inf.Btl. (gep.)
    13.Inf.Geschütz-Kompanie
    14.le.Flak.Kp.(Sf)
    15.Aufkl.-Kompanie (mot.)
    16.Pionier-Kompanie
SS-Panzer-Regiment 12
    I.SS-Pz.Abt.
        Stabs-Kompanie
        Panzer-Flak-Zug (12 Flakpanzer 38(t))
        1.-4.Pz.Kp. (each with 17 Panther tanks)
        Versorgungs-Kompanie
    II.SS-Pz.Abt.
        Stabs-Kompanie
        Panzer-Flak-Zug (3 Flakpanzer IV)
    5.-9.Pz.Kp. (each with 22 PzKpfw IV tanks)
        Panzer-Werkstatt-Kompanie
SS-Panzer-Artillerie-Regiment 12
    Stabs-Batterie (mot.)
    I.SS-Artillerie-Abteilung (Sf)
        Stabs-Batterie (mot.)
        1.-2.Batterie (Sf) (6 Sd Kfz 124 'Wespe')
        3.Batterie (Sf) (6 Sd Kfz 165 'Hummel')
    II.SS-Artillerie-Abteilung (mot.)
        Stabs-Batterie
        4.-6.Batterie (105mm light howitzers)
    III.SS-Artillerie-Abteilung (mot.)
        Stabs-Batterie
        7.-9.Batterie (150mm howitzers)
        10.Batterie (100mm guns)
SS-Werfer-Abt.(mot.) 12
    Stabs-Batterie
    1.-4.Nebelwerfer-Batterie (mot.) (150mm)
    le.Nebelwerfer-Kolonne (mot.)
SS-Panzer-Jäger-Abteilung 12
    Stabs-Kompanie (Sf)
    1.-3.Pz.Jg.Kompanie (Sf)

SS-Flak-Abteilung (mot.) 12
    Stab
    1.Flak-Batterie (mot.) (9 Sdkfz 7/2 with 3,7 cm Flak)
    2.-4.Flak-Batterie (mot.) (each with 4 88mmguns and 3 20mm guns)
    Flak-Scheinwerfer-Staffel (4 60cm searchlights)
    Le.Kraftwagen-Kolonne (mot.)
SS-Panzer-Nachrichten-Abteilung 12
    Stab
    Pz.Fernsprech-Kompanie
    Pz.Funk-Kompanie
    Leichte Nachrichten-Kolonne
SS-Panzer-Aufklärungs-Abteilung 12
    Stabs-Kompanie
    1.-4.Panzer-Späh-Kompanie
    5.Pz.Aufkl.Kompanie
    Versorgungs-Kompanie
SS-Panzer-Pionier-Btl.12
    Stab
    1.Pz.Pi.Kompanie
    2.-3.Pi.Kompanie (mot.)
    Pz.-Brücken-Kol. (Brückengerät 'K')
    Pz.-Brücken-Kol. (Brückengerät 'B')
SS-Division-Nachschub-Truppen (mot.) 12
    Stab
    1.-7.Kraftwagen-Kompanie
    Nachschub-Kompanie
SS-Panzer-Instandsetzungs-Abteilung 12
    Stab
    1.-4.Werstatt-Kompanie (mot.)
    Ersatzteil-Kolonne
SS-Wirtschaft-Bataillon 12
    Stab
        Schlächterei-Kompanie
        Bäckerei-Kompanie
        Verpflegungs-Amt
    Feldpostamt
SS-Sanitäts-*Abteilung 12*
    Stab
    1.-2-Sanitäts-Kompanie (mot.)
    Feldlazarett
    1.-3.Krankenkraftwagen-Zug
SS-Feldersatz-Bataillon 12
    Stab
    1.-5.Kompanie

Invasion

Around midnight on June 5, 1944, news began to arrive at divisional headquarters of paratroopers landing south of the coastal area. I.SS-Panzerkorps, for its part, did not receive any orders or reports. At approximately 0230, the division alerted all its units notwithstanding the lack of guidance from above. SS-Hstuf. Gerd Freiherr von Reitzenstein, an officer of the SS-Aufklärungs-Abteilung, reported: "June 6, 1944. Alert for all units at approximately 0200. Order to move immediately to the designated points. It was still dark when the Aufklärungs-Abteilung started to move. At around 0400, the vehicles took up position at selected crossroads, under the protection of the Flak pieces."

By around 0400, all units of the division were ready for action: SS-Pz.Gren.Rgt.25 began reconnaissance of the Caen area, while the divisional command communicated the alert status to the corps, without yet receiving any orders or information about what was happening. The troops of 716. and 711.Inf.Div., together with those of 21.Pz.Div., located near the bridges of Bénouville and east of the Orne River, began engaging Allied paratroopers who had landed in the area.

A PzKpfw IV and Hitlerjugend motorcyclists on the march. (NARA)

At 0445 am on June 6, 1944, the Supreme Command West (Oberbefehlshaber West) requested the intervention of the Hitlerjugend division, officially still in reserve, and of the 711 Infanterie-Division for possible use at the drop zones. However, the official order did not arrive until 1430, that is ten hours later, an unacceptable delay. In the meantime, following the arrival of the Allied paratroopers in the 711. Inf.Div. sector, 15.Armee HQ instructed: "the 12.SS-Panzer-Division, without neglecting its OKW reserve task, must immediately conduct reconnaissance in the area of 711. Infanterie-Division and observe the sector for a possible enemy landing from the air."

Ten minutes later, Panzergruppe West issued marching orders to Hitlerjugend, the 711.Inf.Div., and the 17.SS-Pz.Gren.Div. "GvB." 12.SS.Division HQ in turn passed the order down to its Aufklärungsabteilung. The commander of 1.Panzerspäh-Kompanie, the company equipped with armored cars, SS-Ostuf. Peter Hansmann, recalled:

> It was about 0230. The phone in the gatehouse rang. My aide, SS-Ostuf. Kurt Buchheim, after hearing the codeword for the warning of the beginning of the invasion, called me on the phone to speak with the commander of our unit, SS-Stubaf. Gerd Bremer. I was then ordered to get to the command post in 15 minutes with ten reconnaissance vehicles and two teams of motorcycle riflemen. The rest of the company had to remain alert and ready to move.
>
> I called my NCOs: "As motorized scouts we must act quickly but with caution, we must look everywhere and not be seen, if possible. We must report to our commander where and how the enemy is located. Our light machine guns are used above all to defend us and remember, that if you use them, you will be immediately

A Hitlerjugend motorized column on the move. In the foreground is a Kubelwagen with the divisional insignia clearly visible on the right rear fender. In front of the motorcyclists is an SdKfz 250/1 and immediately in front of that a Panther. (NARA)

identified by the enemy. And you don't sit in a Tiger tank! Pay particular attention along the way to possible ambushes by partisans, which have recently become more and more frequent. Marching sequence: a team of motorcycle riflemen, eight- and four-wheeled armored cars, at a distance of about 50 meters, another team of motorcycle riflemen as a rear guard. Destination: the Abteilung command post."

After about 15 minutes we reached the command post and I reported to the commander, SS-Stubaf. Bremer. I received information on enemy air landings along the coastal area and behind our defensive positions, from the area west of the mouth of the Seine in Carentan ... Our recon teams began their reconnaissance around 0400 ... At 1100, I sent a report: "All along the coast, from Arromanches Bay to the west, passing through the mouth of the Orne River to the east, ships of all kinds are landing troops and firing at our coastal defenses. Tough fighting is taking place along the Courseulles–St. Aubin coastal road."

A 2cm SS Flakvierling in Normandy.

At 0500, 15.Armee reported to Heeresgruppe that Allied paratroopers were continuing to land in the Houlgate area. Half an hour later, Armee requested that the division take action as soon as possible. However, Generalleutnant Speidel first wanted to discuss the situation with Supreme Command West. Ten minutes later, Generalmajor Pemsel, commander of 7.Armee, reported that the situation east of the Orne River was apparently calm, but that the enemy was still holding the bridge at Bénouville. Speidel, after finally speaking with General Blumentritt, commander of Supreme Command West, learned that Heeresgruppe had planned to deploy Hitlerjugend troops on both sides of Lisieux as soon as possible. Supreme Command West then made the decision to assign the Hitlerjugend to Heeresgruppe D, without waiting for the approval of the OKH, then ordered the transfer of the division to the 711.Div. sector, in order to immediately engage paratroops that had landed in the Bernay–Lisieux–Vimoutiers area.

The transfer order was sent from Heeresgruppe to Panzergruppe West at 0550. The division was to make contact immediately with the general headquarters of the LXXXI. Armeekorps in Rouen and with the 711.Inf.Div. in Le Quesnay. At the same time the Flak companies of SS-Pz.Gr.Rgt.26 were transferred back to the division, having been engaged in the antiaircraft defense of the Seine crossings at Elbeuf and Gaillon. Between 0630 and 0700, the transfer order arrived at the divisional headquarters, taking the staff by surprise: Hitlerjugend had in fact already deployed most of its advanced units, including the entire

A pair of 3./SS-Pz.Rgt.12 Panthers on the march. In the foreground is SS-Ustuf. Rolf Jauch. (SS-PK Woscidlo)

SS-Stubaf. Hans Waldmüller.

armored regiment, north of the Bernay–Lisieux line. According to the order received from Heeresgruppe, the tanks would have to travel initially southwest and then north-northwest, in order to reach the sector of 711.Inf. Div., a useless and time-consuming march in terms of time and fuel. In addition, the division had already prepared a deployment plan on the ground, between the mouths of the Seine and Orne, which thus had to be shelved.

Having to comply with the new provisions, the division found itself with its non-combatant service units forward and had to reorganize itself in an area of only 25 square kilometers. From here there were only two viable roads to the coast. The Lisieux crossing was particularly threatened by attacks from Allied fighter-bombers. The division's chief of staff, SS-Stubaf.

A Hitlerjugend Panther. (NARA)

Hubert Meyer, telephoned his I.SS-Panzerkorps counterpart, SS-Brigdf. Fritz Krämer, to try to have the orders reversed, but in vain, also taking into account that the division, despite being part of I.SS-Panzerkorps, together with the LSSAH, had been temporarily detached from it.

A fresh marching order for the new assembly area was then immediately prepared and passed on to the unit commanders. The war diary of I./SS-Pz.Gr.Rgt. 25 reported that the battalion received the alarm at 0300 and the codeword *Blücher* at 0555. The unit was ready to move as early as 0600. The codeword indicated that the troops had to prepare to move to the designated departure points. The battalion began its march along the designated plan Z road at 1000, after receiving the order by radio from the regimental headquarters. The Flak-Abteilung received the departure order at 0800 together with the instructions for the anti-aircraft defense of the area around Lisieux. The second and fourth batteries, equipped with 8.8cm and 3.7cm pieces respectively, were supposed to cross the river at Les Andelys, but deployed separately. The other units of the division were alerted between 1000 and 1100. The divisional command post (CP) initially remained in Acon as long as the telephone line worked, while another provisional headquarters was set up in Lisieux. The commander of SS-Pz.Gr. Rgt. 25, SS-Staf. Kurt Meyer, began a reconnaissance in the Caen area immediately after the alarm.

During the day, the Oberbefehlshaber West became convinced that the landing of troops from the sea was limited to the strip of beach west of the mouth of the Orne. In addition, 15.Armee had reported to Heeresgruppe at 1020 that a battalion of Allied paratroopers had been routed in the rear of 711.Inf.Div. and 40 prisoners taken. Based on this optimistic information, OOB West ordered "that 12.SS-Pz.Div. had to prepare to move west." The division certainly could not carry out the order given that the troops were already on their

III./SS-Pz.Gr.Rgt.26 SdKfz 251/1 halftracks. (US NARA)

way to the new assembly area. At 1432, OOB West informed Heeresgruppe that the OKW had transferred the Hitlerjugend to 7.Armee. However, it was still to be determined which headquarters the division should answer to. Soon thereafter, Heeresgruppe was informed that the Panzer-Lehr-Division had also been detached from the OKW and that OOB West had advised them to move to the Flers area. The Hitlerjugend and the Pz-Lehr-Division were then assigned to 7.Armee to engage the bridgehead in the sector of the 716. Inf.Div. Army HQ issued the following order through Panzergruppe West:

> 1) 12.SS-Pz.-Div. must be placed immediately north of the Alençon–Carrouges line on both sides of Evrecy, about 8 kilometers southwest of Caen and is initially assigned to LXXXIV.Armeekorps. Its mission is to intercept the enemy units that have just landed in the area west of the sector of the 21.Pz.Div., throw them back toward the sea and annihilate them;

> 2) Pz-Lehr-Division must instead be placed immediately south of the same line and initially must occupy the Flers–Vire area, about 50 kilometers southwest of Caen.

Soon after, it was decided to assign the 21.Pz.Div., the 12.SS-Pz.Div., the Pz-Lehr-Division and the 716.Inf.Div. to I.SS-Pz.Korps and to transfer them to the easterly sector of LXXXIV Armeekorps.

Redeployment of Units

The order from Panzergruppe West to deploy the division to the Caen area arrived at the Hitlerjugend command post at approximately 1700, when part of the division had already

reached the new assembly areas. I./25, led by SS-Stubaf. Hans Waldmüller, had reached Saint-Pierre-des-Ifs, 6 kilometers southwest of Lisieux, around 1300, taking up positions on both sides of the road, with supplies and the rear of the battalion taking positions in Vimoutiers. With most of the troops on the march, no one at the divisional headquarters knew the situation in the Caen area: it was only known that the Allies had dropped paratroopers east of the Orne and west of the mouth, so they had to conduct reconnaissance in the new assembly area and from there to the coast. Arrangements along the way required that, in the new

SS-Stubaf. Karl-Heinz Prinz.

assembly area, SS-Pz.Gr.Rgt.26, commanded by SS-Ostubaf. Monhke, together with the I.Pz.Abteilung, under SS-Stubaf. Jürgensen, were to take position on the right flank of the area, while SS-Pz.Gr.Rgt.26 of SS-Staf. Kurt Meyer with II.Pz.Abteilung led by SS-Stubaf. Prinz was on the left.

During the afternoon, OKW ordered all units to move quickly to take advantage of poor weather conditions. Schweppenburg advised regrouping the panzer divisions only after 2000, to avoid Allied air attacks. Hitlerjugend units had been savaged by Allied *Jabos* during the day, losing several vehicles.

Sturmmann Martin Besel, of I.Zug, 13.Kompanie, SS-Pz.Gr.Rgt.25, remembered: "During our march we were attacked by enemy fighter-bombers. Our commander, 'Panzermeyer,' was lucky on that occasion, jumping out of his vehicle just in time. He threw himself down on the left, while a bomb exploded on the right side, completely destroying his vehicle. The attack was aimed at a bridge which, thank God, remained intact."

Initially it was felt that the Allied air attacks had caused heavy losses, but this was not the case. For example, the divisional escort company reported no casualties during its June 6 march, only damage to vehicles, some of which were soon repaired.

However, even though the Allied air strikes slowed the division's progress to the Caen assembly areas, and in spite of the contradictory orders of the German high command, all Hitlerjugend subunits arrived during the night of June 6/7.

Halftracks resume their march after an air attack.

An SdKfz 251/10 towing a PaK 40 on the Normandy front—always on the lookout for Allied fighter-bombers. (NARA)

| The Battle for Caen Begins

Kurt Meyer had travelled at the head of his regiment to reach the 716. Infanterie-Division CP, located in a bunker in the Folie area. He arrived around midnight on June 6 and met with Generalleutnant Richter and the commander of 21.Pz.Div., Generalmajor Feuchtinger. The situation appeared critical: 716.Inf.Div. had been defeated and the road to Caen was open to Allied forces.

Furthermore, Feuchtinger did not have a clear view of the situation and of the positions of the various *Kampfgruppen* in his division. He reported that there was the possibility that the city and the airfield at Carpiquet were already in the hands of the Allies, which Meyer ascertained was not the case: Carpiquet, Rots, and Buron were still in German hands. Scattered elements of 716.Inf.Div. had been sighted in Buron, while the position of Les Buissons had been captured. As soon as Meyer returned to his CP, housed in a small café in Saint-Germain-la-Blanche-Herbe, west of the Caen exit, he received a call from SS-Brigdf. Witt, who informed Meyer of the I.SS-Pz.Korp order, that 21.Pz.Div. should attack to the left of the front, at 1600 on June 7, to throw the enemy back into the sea. Witt emphasized that the area around the Carpiquet airport should be protected under all circumstances.

A Hitlerjugend column after an Allied *Jabo* attack.

Meyer Prepares

At 0300, Meyer issued orders to his battalion commanders for a regimental attack against the advancing Allied troops. I.Bataillon was positioned on the right flank of the northerly advance and II.Bataillon on the left. I.Bataillon had to regroup on the left flank of 21.Pz.Div. between Epron and La Folie, II.Bataillon at Bitot, and III.Bataillon was placed in reserve southeast of Franqueville, south of the Caen–Bayeux road. III.Artillerie-Abteilung had to take a position so as to be able to provide fire support to the entire regimental attack, while a battery of heavy guns was to cooperate with each battalion.

Meyer, with the III.Artillerie-Abteilung commander, SS-Stubaf. Bartling, placed his CP in Ardenne Abbey, while the division moved its command to the southwestern exit of Caen, in the Venoix district, along the Caen–Villers-Bocage road. The SS grenadiers marched all night to reach their start line. Meyer commented:

> The commander of I. Bataillon came to report [to the CP]. I was quickly briefed on the situation; we knew that a difficult confrontation was ahead of us. The men of the battalion had jumped from the vehicles and trucks, disappearing into the darkness. No vehicle crossed the city, everyone headed south … The grenadiers were approaching. Very calmly, without letting emotions show but with the firm determination to be ready for their baptism of fire.

Around 0900, Meyer arrived in his Kubelwagen at the Abbey after avoiding the Allied fighter-bombers that infested the area. Bartling advised that the artillery was in position and ready to open fire. The first 50 panzers started arriving around 1000, ready for action. Prinz advised that the balance would only arrived later that day, into the evening. The three battalions confirmed they were all on their start lines.

Coat of Arms

The divisional coat of arms was expressly chosen in view of incorporation of the unit into I.SS-Panzerkorps, which also included LSSAH. The emblem was the result of a mini-competition that began on November 10, 1943, and was won by SS-Rottenführer Franz Lang of Abteilung V (transport) of the divisional staff. All vehicles in the division, from motorbikes to Panther tanks, received the emblem painted in white. The members of the division enthusiastically welcomed the choice of the emblem, which made them feel close to their Leibstandarte comrades.

The Enemy Prepares

Meanwhile, the Allies were also preparing to attack Caen, in particular the British 3rd Infantry Division, ready to attack the sector assigned to 21.Pz.Div., whose right flank bordered the Hitlerjugend sector. The 2nd Battalion, Royal Ulster Rifles, reinforced by a tank company from the East Riding Yeomanry, was advancing behind positions of the 1st Battalion, King's Own Scottish Borderers at Le Mesnil, in front of I./SS -Pz.Gr.Rgt.25. The vanguard of the 9th Canadian Infantry Brigade, the Nova Scotia Highlanders and the 27th Armored Regiment (Sherbrooke Fusiliers Regiment), regrouped on the morning of June 7, with the aim of reaching Carpiquet airfield.

At Villons-les-Buissons, the Canadians came under fire from Flak and PaK pieces, but after a pincer attack, the position was cleared. Around noon, the village of Buron, defended by isolated elements of 716.Inf.Div., fell.

Meyer received the news that a large Allied armored formation was gathering south of Colomby-sur-Thaon. He gave the order to wait until the enemy was in range before opening fire. At the same time, SS-Ustuf. Porsch took four PzKpfw IVs along the Franqueville–Authie

Artillery observers in the bell tower of the Abbey of Ardenne. (NARA)

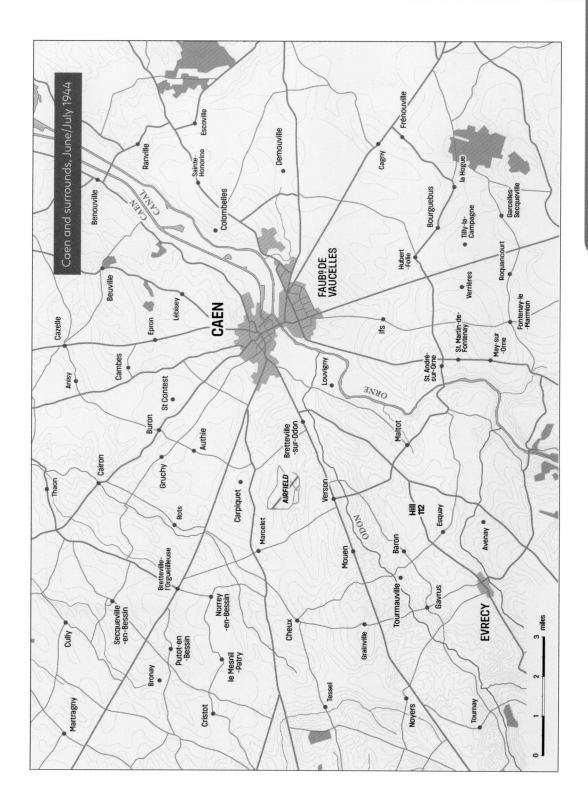

Caen and surrounds, June/July 1944

CAEN
CANAL
CAEN
FAUB. DE VAUCELLES
ORNE
ODON
AIRFIELD
Hill 112
EVRECY

Martragny
Cully
Thaon
Cairon
Anisy
Cazelle
Beuville
Benouville
Ranville
Escoville
Sainte-Honorine
Colombelles
Demouville
Cambes
St Contest
Buron
Gruchy
Epron
Lébisey
Cagny
Frénouville
Bronay
Rots
Authie
Bourguebus
la Hogue
Secqueville-en-Bessin
Carpiquet
Hubert-Folie
Tilly-la-Campagne
Garcelles-Secqueville
Bretteville-l'Orgueilleuse
Marcelet
Bretteville-sur-Odon
Ifs
Verrières
Roquancourt
Cristot
Putot-en-Bessin
Norrey-en-Bessin
Louvigny
St. Martin-de-Fontenay
Fontenay-le-Marmion
le Mesnil-Patry
Verson
Baron
Maltot
St. André-sur-Orne
May-sur-Orne
Cheux
Mouen
Tourmauville
Tessel
Grainville
Gavrus
Esquay
Avenay
Noyers
Tournay

0   1   2   3 miles

Preparation for the attack of June 7, in the courtyard of the Abbey of Ardenne. From left: SS-Stubaf. Erick Urbanitz, commander of I.(gep)/SS-Pz.Art.Rgt.12; SS-Stubaf. Karl-Heinz Prinz, commander of II./SS-Pz.Rgt.12; and SS-Stubaf. Karl Bartling, commander of II./SS-Pz.art.Rgt.12.

road but at around 1440 he unexpectedly ran into the Sherbrooke Fusiliers' Shermans advancing from Authie. In the brief firefight that followed, three of his panzers were lost.

Meyer immediately ordered the CO SS-Pz.Rgt.12, SS-Ostubaf. Max Wünsche, and the CO III./25, SS-Ostubaf. Karl-Heinz Milius, to counterattack on the Allied flank. Wünsche transmitted the order: *"Achtung, Panzer Marsch!"* Taken by surprise, within minutes ten Shermans were knocked out for the loss of five PzKpfw IVs. The panzers with *Panzergrenadieren* of 9.Kompanie, then took Authie, before advancing on Buron.

SS-Sturmmann Hans Fenn, gunner in I.Zug, 6.Pz.Kp., recalled:

> Ostuf. Gasch, came to us, taking command of the point platoon, I .Zug. We delivered some prisoners to the grenadiers without getting off our panzers, then continued to advance, only to find ourselves shortly after in a flat open area under fire from Canadian antitank guns. Four of my platoon tanks were destroyed. We, in the fifth tank, took a direct hit between the side and the turret as we attempted to escape the fire of the enemy antitank guns. We were unable to hit Canadian fire positions at a distance of 1,500, 2,000 meters. A shell passed through the legs of my commander, Oscha. Esser, but he managed to get out of the turret. Since it was a phosphorus grenade, the whole tank caught fire. Somehow, I managed to get out through the loader's hatch, falling on the ground half burned, I went back to our grenadiers who followed behind. Our medical NCO took me to the field hospital in a car.

SS-Ostubaf. Karl-Heinz Milius, left.

PzKpfw IV "536" advances to action.

Hitlerjugend grenadiers storm enemy positions.

The Canadian commander ordered his companies to adopt a defensive position north of Authie as SS-Pz.Gr.Rgt.25 and the two Panzer companies attacked Buron and Gruchy supported by artillery fire directed by SS-Stubaf. Bartling from the Ardenne Abbey tower.

A Company, North Nova Scotia Highlanders, was overwhelmed north of Authie; however, German units approaching the southern outskirts of Buron were stopped by a heavy barrage of Canadian artillery, causing losses among the panzers and the Panzergrenadieren grenadiers. SS-Sturmmann Vasold:

> We attacked Buron with the remaining panzers, engaged in house-to-house fighting. Numerous prisoners were captured. Under the incessant fire of enemy heavy machine guns, we were forced to relinquish ground again to the enemy. There was no possibility of continuing; we had to retreat again, under the protection of one of our panzers.

At around 1500, Meyer ordered I. and II.Bataillone to attack. II.Bataillon was exposed to enemy fire on its left wing, from the North Nova Scotia and the 27th Armored Regiment. The right wing was attacked by the 2nd Royal Ulster Regiment, supported by the East Riding Yeomanry tanks, which attacked from Le Mesnil in the direction of Cambes. Meanwhile the panzers from Authie began arriving.

A young Hitlerjugend machine-gunner armed with an MG-42, dressed in an M44 camouflage uniform. (Hubert Meyer collection)

En route Saint-Contest was taken without difficulty. However three Canadian tanks suddenly appeared. SS-Stubaf. Scappini was seriously wounded. Meyer, who had arrived on the spot on a motorcycle, ordered SS-Hstuf. Schrott to assume command of II./SS-Pz.GR.25. The three enemy tanks retreated, with the battalion then taking Malon and Galmanche without encountering too much resistance, thwarted only by Allied artillery fire.

SS-Stubaf. Hans Waldmüller's I.Bataillon regrouped on the right of II.Bataillon, having as its first objective Anguerny, 9 kilometers north of Caen. The attack began at 1615; however, at a wooded area north of Cambes, Sherman tanks appeared on the left of the village, in front of the grenadiers, opening fire. In the shelter of the trees, the grenadiers stalled as Allied artillery and mortars opened fire on them, soon joined by fighter-bombers.

SS-Schütze Emil Werner of 3.Kompanie recalled:

> The time came for the attack on Cambes. We could see the village very well from our position. On reaching its outskirts, we were greeted by the fire of the enemy infantry. We launched an attack on a church, where some enemy snipers had holed up. Shortly after, I saw the first comrade of my company, SS-Grenadier Rühl, fall, hit by a bullet in the head. The situation immediately became critical. My commander was wounded in the arm and had to be evacuated. SS-Grenadier Grosse of Hamburg jumped behind me toward some bushes with his submachine gun pointed, shouting, "Hands up!": immediately, two British soldiers came out with their hands raised. Grosse was later decorated with Iron Cross. Ustuf. Gschaider approached me soon after and we both took cover behind an abandoned Heer truck under a tree. Gschaider then pointed to a house, saying: "Werner,

Paula, a Hitlerjugend PzKpfw IV.

Hitlerjugend grenadiers move to assault enemy positions.

shoot at it!" As I opened fire, Gschaider was hit by an explosive bullet in his face. He could no longer speak and had to be evacuated. A few seconds later, Uscha. Hatzke yelled at me: "Let's go on!"

The four 8.Pz.Kp panzers began their attack—one was left behind due to a mechanical problem—and advanced from the west of Malon, identifying several enemy positions to the west of the wooded area north of Cambes. SS-Ostuf. Siegel:

I was in the lead with my panzer. Stopping to be able to shoot became more and more risky. So, I went along the edge of the forest to be more sheltered. A shell exploded in the trees causing numerous branches to fall on my panzer, completely limiting my visibility. At the same time, two of my vehicles were moving behind me. Both were hit when they stopped to open fire. The fourth panzer fell into a crater, getting stuck. Our panzers were put out of action even before we engaged in any action.

Meanwhile, the *Panzergrenadieren* had destroyed three Shermans with Panzerfausts. SS-Uscha. Helmut Stöcker of the Schwere Infanteriegeschütz Kompanie, the heavy infantry gun company, which supported the attack, stated:

The attack was launched quickly by the infantry. Due to the short range of our guns, we had to advance with the infantry, who were attacking without armored support. Everywhere, there was a massive barrage that blocked our advance. We were ahead of Cambes, on open ground with our vehicles and guns. In order to allow the infantry to continue moving forward, our platoon moved toward

A Hitlerjugend grenadier armed with a Panzerfaust.

A schwere Infanterie Geschütz 33 of SS-Pz.Gren.Rgt.25.

Cambes. We had no other choice and would probably be routed within minutes. After having reached Cambes, we took up positions in a ditch: we could hear the sound of tracks coming from the village. About 50 meters in front of us, a Sherman suddenly emerged from a side street. stopped at an intersection and sighted us and our guns. The turret of the tank turned towards us and before we knew what was happening, the first shot landed on us. We were saved by jumping to the shelter of a half-destroyed farmhouse. The next shot fell among our guns and tow vehicles. We were lucky because it was probably an antitank shell and not an explosive shell. Already loaded with our material, we didn't have any antitank weapons with us, but luckily a I./25 grenadier arrived with a Panzerfaust. Thanks to a well-aimed shot, the Sherman was hit and destroyed, thus blocking the main intersection in the village.

The Ulster Rifles came under fire from German artillery and mortars as they attempted to access the village of Le Mesnil and were forced to retreat. I. Bataillon was unable to pursue the retreating enemy because the entire wooded area was being subjected to a massive barrage by the Allied artillery and mortars. German artillery support was lost when the advanced observer was killed. SS-Stubaf. Waldmüller then decided to disengage and take up defensive positions on the southern side of Cambes. However, these new positions were immediately subjected to bombardment by Allied artillery.

SS-Pz.Gren.Rgt.25 grenadiers on a troop transport halftrack. (NARA)

A PzKpfw IV covered in foliage, in an ambush position.

SS-Stubaf. Waldmüller (right) in a field south of Cambes, plans a deployment with two Waffen-SS officers.

At 1600, the Divisionbegleitkompanie, the divisional escort company, entered Rots from southeast, coming under enemy fire, a sign that the bridge over the River Mue at Rots was occupied by the enemy. West of the Mue, the enemy had already crossed the Caen–Bayeux road.

From the Ardenne Abbey tower, Meyer spotted enemy tanks approaching Bretteville-l'Orgeilleuse from the north and west of the crest of Mue, a serious threat to his exposed left flank. I./25 therefore had to move south of Cambes while an armored counterattack on Buron was underway.

At the same time, the Canadian 9th Infantry Brigade ordered the North Nova Scotia Highlanders to recapture Le Buissons but a German counterattack at the same time occupied Buron and forced the Canadians to retreat while III./25 panzers (SS-Ostuf. Helmut Bando) secured the northern side of Gruchy. SS-Pz.Rgt.12 and SS-Pz.Gr.Rgt.25 dug in for the night along a line that ran from Caen–Luc-sur-Mer station to Route Nationale 13. The right wing of the I.Bataillon was located along the railway line south of Cambes, where a tenuous connection with the 21.Panzer-Division had been established.

SS-Pz.Gr. Rgt. 25 had successfully repelled the British and Canadians, blocking them north and northwest of Caen, also managing to repel the forward armored units that had pushed as far as the airfield at Carpiquet, inflicting heavy losses on the enemy. German losses were also considerable, mainly due to enemy artillery fire. North Nova Scotia alone reported 242 casualties, 21 tanks destroyed and another seven damaged. SS-Pz.Rgt.12 lost nine PzKpfw IVs.

Hitlerjugend grenadiers pass through a town during the fighting north of Caen. (NARA)

Hitlerjugend grenadiers near the Ardenne Abbey, awaiting orders. (NARA)

The Action of SS-Pz.Aufkl.Abt.12

SS-Pz.Aufkl.Abt.12 was engaged farther west, against units of the British 50th Northumbrian Division while leading units of the British 69th Brigade arrived at the Caen–Bayeux road. During the night of June 6/7, elements of SS-Pz.Aufkl.Abt.12 reached Verson area, 7 kilometers southwest of Caen. As soon as dawn broke, recon patrols went into action but collided with Allied units on the outskirts near the Bretteville-l'Orgeilleuse railway station toward noon. Another patrol, also in eight-wheeled vehicles, vanished into thin air northwest of Caen.

An armored patrol from Le Mesnil, led by SS-Oscha. Karl Jura, intercepted some Canadian jeeps south of Pûtot. At Cristot, at the Abteilung CP, he was ordered to undertake reconnaissance in a northwesterly direction toward Seoul beyond Route Nationale 13, from Caen to Bayeux. At Ducy elements of the Durham Light Infantry were encountered for the first time and driven back.

The bulk of SS-Pz.Aufkl.Abt.12 meanwhile continued to Tilly-sur-Seulles during the morning of June 7, advancing on the Le Mesnil-Patry–Cristot road axis. Attacks by Allied fighter-bombers slowed the march, as did sporadic attacks by enemy infantry. The Abteilung then assumed a defensive position by preparing a series of fortified strongpoints, on a line that extended from La Rue (southeast of Audrieu) through the northern part of Audrieu to the area west of Hill 103 (southwest of Audrieu).

In Profile:
Jagdpanzer IV/70 of
12.SS-Pz.Div. Hitlerjugend

Technical specifications

Crew: 4
Weight: 25,800 kg (28.44 tons)
Engine: Maybach HL 120 petrol engine, 265 hp

Dimensions:
- Length: 8.58m (31'6")
- Width: 2.93m (9'7")
- Height: 1.96m (6'5")

Performance:
- Maximum speed (on road): 35 km/h (20.5 mph)
- Range (on road): 214km (133 miles)
- Ford 1.2m (3'11"); slope 57%, step 0.6m (2'); trench 2.3m (7'6")

The 1942 campaigns led German designers to test new self-propelled anti-tank guns fitted with a gun larger than those mounted on the Sturmgeschütz, and the choice was the long version of the 7.5cm gun that was already in use on the Panther tank. Mounting that gun on the hull of a Sturmgeschütz III, however, would require extensive and time-consuming modifications, so it was decided to use the larger chassis of the PzKpfw IV. Design began in 1943 and led to development of the Jagdpanzer IV Ausf. F für PaK 39 7.5cm, also known as the Panzerjäger 39. Nevertheless, when the first examples were ready, the Jagdpanzer had to use a 4.8cm gun because the 7.5cm guns were being used on the Panthers on a priority basis. The first Jagdpanzer IV vehicles made their appearance in October 1943 with the suspension and engine of the PzKpfw IV, while they used the new armored casemate with angled side plates; the hull silhouette was much lower than the hull/turret combination of the Panzer IV. The gun was mounted well forward and was well protected by a mantlet. The Jagdpanzer quickly became famous and was widely requested by many units because of its low silhouette and armored casemate. The gun was powerful enough to deal with most enemy tanks it encountered. Likewise, the secondary armament, consisting of two MG 34 or MG 42 machine guns proved to be very effective. Despite the German armor crews who felt that it was quite suitable as it was and did not need a more powerful gun, Hitler himself decreed that an even longer 7.5cm gun should be mounted on the vehicle. It was thus that in 1944 the first Jagdpanzer IV mit Stuk. 42 7.5cm made its appearance with the new gun. However, its construction required production lines to be modified, resulting in a third version of the Jagdpanzer IV, designated Panzer IV/70 Zwischenlösung (intermediate solution) which entered production in late 1944. The Jagdpanzer IVs proved themselves on the battlefield, but the excessive weight of the long gun barrel put too much stress on the front of the vehicle, to the point that the front rubber-tired wheels had to be replaced by steel ones.

However, the rest of I./26 under SS-Hstuf. Helmut Eggert had managed to recapture Rots on its own but a yawning gap had developed between it and its two wayward companies south of Norrey. Some Panthers took up ambush positions on the outskirts of Bretteville while the Divisionbegleitkompanie took control of the road bridge over the Mue near Le Bourg to prevent the Allies forcing the gap.

That same day, June 9, Panzergruppe West ordered Hitlerjugend to conduct a night attack to capture Norrey, which was strongly defended. Hauptmann Lüdemann's 3./SS-Pz. Rgt.12 with 12 tanks but without artillery hoped that surprise might reduce the enemy. However, as the Panthers advanced across the open fields to their target, Canadian tanks hidden from sight brought their guns to bear. One after another, the Panthers caught fire, their crews incinerated. Six of the 12 were destroyed outright, the others falling back in disarray. The Canadians machine-gunned the few survivors. More serious for Hitlerjugend, it left a Canadian fortified position wedged between SS-Pz.Gr.Rgt.25 and SS-Pz.Gr.Rgt.26 to the south.

The Pioneers Attack

During the night of June 10/11, the division's pioneer battalion, under SS-Stubaf. Siegfried Müller, the only unit that had seen no action, was ordered to eliminate the dangerous Canadian salient, together with SS-Pz.Gr.Rgt.26; the German pioneers were considered elite infantry, specialized in assault operations. Under the cover of darkness, the pioneer assault teams took up their start positions south of Norrey, The SS units attempted to approach the Canadian positions in silence, but were discovered nonetheless and a massive barrage of mortars and artillery was immediately unleashed.

Oberleutnant Toll's company managed to reach the outskirts of the village, sheltering as best it could in the local gullies, while the SS pioneers began responding to the enemy fire. As soon as enemy fire seemed to wane, the Germans renewed their attack but the Canadians responded with machine guns, killing many of the SS pioneers, including Toll who died of his wounds soon after being hit.

What was left of the company fell back, bringing all their wounded with them. southwest of Norrey. Command of the company then passed to

Hitlerjugend pioneers building defensive positions.

June 9, 1944, 3.Pz.Kp Panthers cross the rue de la Villeneuve, in Rots. In the foreground is a scout from 15.(Aufkl).Kp/SS-Pz.Gr.Rgt.25 in his Schwimmwagen. (NARA)

SS-Ustuf. Bruno Asmus. The attack by the other pioneer companies was also unsuccessful, again due to the intense barrage by the Canadians. Pioneer losses were significant: three officers, three NCOs, and 22 soldiers killed.

SS-Pz.Gr.Rgt.25 onto the Defensive

After its attack, SS-Pz.Gr.Rgt.25 went onto the defensive, while the Canadians had already crossed the Caen–Bayeux road, west of the Mue ridge to resume their attack in the sector occupied by Meyer's men, with the aim of capturing Caen. However, German artillery managed to stem the tide.

On June 8, British artillery bombarded the regiment's positions followed by infantry attacks, with tank support, against I. and II.Bataillone: at least two Allied tanks were destroyed by antitank guns. On June 9, the Royal Ulsters attacked again, moving from Anisy in the afternoon, with the aim of seizing Cambes: to support it was the 3rd Division artillery and a cruiser offshore. However, when the Ulsters got to within a kilometer of their target, they sustained concentrated German artillery, mortar, and machine-gun fire, suffering serious casualties.

Iron Crosses for young SS grenadiers. (Hugh Page Taylor collection)

German casualties were as heavy as the Allies. During the fighting on June 9, SS-Ostuf, Heinz-Hugo John fell in combat. He had participated in the attack on June 7, as commander of I Zug, 7.Pz.Kp. After SS-Hstuf. Heinrich Bräcker was wounded, he had assumed command of the company. In the unit's daily report, his loss was reported:

SS-Ostuf. Heinz John was killed in action on June 9, 1944 at around 8:00 pm, near La Folie, as commander of a company of 7./SS-Pz.Rgt.12. The mission of the company was to protect the positions from attacks by enemy tanks and infantry. The area where the company had gathered suddenly came under mortar fire. Ostuf. John received the radio order to go to the Abteilung command post to receive further orders. Just as the Ostuf. was about to jump out of the Panzer, a direct shot hit the radio operator's hatch. A large piece of shrapnel hit Ostuf. John in the spine, killing him instantly. The radio operator, SS-Sturmmann Mende and the loader, SS-Schütze Noa were also killed. The driver and gunner managed to evacuate the vehicle in time and reach the Abteilung command post.

A 15./25 SS grenadier in Rots.

| The Second Battle for Caen

On June 11, 1944, SS-Brigdf. Witt inspected the men of SS-Aufkl. Abt.12, accompanied by the commander, SS-Stubaf. Gerd Bremer. He also presented awards to the SS scouts. SS-Hstuf. Freiherr Gerd von Reitzenstein, CO 5./SS-Pz.Aufkl.Abt.12, reported to the two commanders: losses caused by mortar fire and Allied fighter-bombers had been high.

Most unit commanders were out of action and companies were down to half the strength. The enemy had sent tank-supported patrols against the scouts' positions, but they had been driven back by antitank fire. Subsequently, the 69th Infantry Brigade attacked in the direction of Saint-Pierre, Cristot, and the forests east of Caen, supported by tanks, and immediately clashed with Hitlerjugend recon patrols, unleashing furious firefights in the forests. In the afternoon, Allied troops reached the area northeast of Les Hauts Vents, but found themselves

Hitlerjugend grenadiers taking orders from their bandaged officer.

A Hitlerjugend antitank gun opens fire. (NARA)

under a violent barrage west of Cristot. However, the British units managed to continue in the direction of Hill 102. Other Allied units, south of the same hill, suffered heavy losses after being involved in bitter fighting.

At 1720, another Allied armored attack began, accompanied by the 6th Green Howards. Waiting to open fire, the German halftrack machine-gunners cut down the Green Howard infantry, causing considerable casualties. The British attack finally faltered when the lead Sherman was destroyed by a 7.5cm antitank gun. The reserve Panther company then arrived and drove the British back, who left at least 250 dead and seven tanks on the field.

As soon as it got dark, the 7th Green Howards withdrew to northwest of Brouay but the advance of the 5th East Yorks on Saint-Pierre triggered a counterattack by II./Pz.-Lehr-Rgt.130 who penetrated British positions on Hill 103 northeast of Tilly-sur-Seulles. Two panzers were destroyed and the rest were driven back. At the same time, the 22nd Armoured Brigade, 7th Armoured Division captured Vérrieres, about a kilometer northeast of Lingèvre.

A Hitlerjugend motorcyclist in Normandy.

The Attack on Le Mesnil-Patry

The 3rd Canadian Infantry Division had planned an attack with the 2nd Canadian Armoured Brigade for June 12: its goal was to conquer the heights south of Cheux (Hill 107). As a precondition for this attack, there was a need to clear the Mue valley near Rots by June 11. To support the 69th Infantry Brigade attack against the Brouay–Cristot sector, both attacks were planned for June 11. At dawn of that fateful date, the 2nd Canadian Armoured Brigade received the order to launch the attack against Hill 107 south of Cheux, engaging the 6th Armoured Regiment, another armored unit, and the Queen's Own Rifles of Canada, an infantry battalion. The first objective was to take Le Mesnil-Patry, then turn left, pass through Haute du Bosq and take control of the hills south of Cheux. However, Hitlerjugend radio intercepts allowed the SS units to prepare.

The attack began at 1430 and immediately saw the SS pioneers engaged in fierce battles with Canadian infantry and tanks, using antitank rifles, Panzerfausts, and magnetic mines. The commander of 8.Pz.Kp., SS-Ostuf. Hans Siegel, at his CP south of Fontenay, received a request for assistance from SS-Ostubaf. Mohnke, CO SS-Pz.Gr.Rgt.26, that was facing an Allied armored attack at Le Mesnil. Siegel, along with 1.Pionier-Kompanie, set up an ambush about a kilometer south of Le Mesnil and duly engaged Canadian tanks and infantry, destroying at least one squadron of Allied tanks. Siegel reported:

> During a stop during the march to scout the area, some grenadiers showed us where the enemy was, a sign that the situation was particularly serious. The hatches were closed and the guns were put into firing position. A hedge still obstructed our field of vision to the left. When all was clearer, I found myself in the midst of our own infantry and at the same time saw numerous Shermans approaching right in front of them and our flank was exposed.

A Hitlerjugend antitank position on the outskirts of Le Mesnil-Patry.

"Enemy tank left, nine o'clock, 200 meters, open fire!"

Within minutes, four or five Allied tanks were burning. The last one, however, was only spotted at the last moment, when it was about 100 meters away from us and its turret was turning in our direction.

"Enemy tank left, 10 o'clock, 100 meters!"

Tank against tank, almost on top of us, when I saw it through the periscope. Then an explosion, the fire of our 7.5cm cannon. The other tank exploded. The command panzer managed to destroy two more Shermans. My tank was then hit by antitank fire, so I moved it into firing position but it then suffered a direct hit. The crew abandoned the vehicle, except for the radio operator who was killed instantly. The tank started burning.

Hitlerjugend Panther and grenadiers in the streets of Rots. (*Illustrierte Beobachter*)

A Hitlerjugend Steyr 1500A burns following an Allied air raid.

The Fighting for Rots

The village of Rots had been captured on June 9. It was then heavily reinforced by pioneers and infantry, with several PaK guns from SS-Hstuf. Helmut Eggert's unit. SS-Hstuf. Hans Pfeiffer was back in the fray with several Panthers on hand. These advanced German positions profoundly threatened the Canadian flank in Norrey, Bretteville, and Putot, therefore, the 3rd Canadian Division was ordered to eliminate them.

For the attack, the 8th Canadian Infantry Brigade deployed the 46th Royal Marine Commando, reinforced by a company of the 10th Canadian Armoured Regiment. The Allied units had to advance along the Mue valley from north to south, repel the enemy and clear the valley itself. The two infantry battalions, de la Chauderie and North Shore, were to reduce the villages in the valley before the attack by the Royal Marines. On June 10, German positions were subjected to a massive artillery bombardment. Then tanks were sighted, but no attacks were recorded. On the morning of June 11, another Allied artillery bombardment

A Hitlerjugend MG 42 defensive position. (NARA)

was unleashed, as a dozen Shermans with supporting infantry were spotted on the right flank of the Mue valley. They ended up in the crosshairs of a Panther well sited near a church.

The Royal Marines, along with the Shermans, penetrated the north of Rots. German losses were heavy. The CO Divisionbegleitkompanie, SS-Ostuf. Guntrum, with two squads and some Panthers, launched a counterattack, managing to free part of the village. The Panthers destroyed six Shermans and about 40 prisoners were taken.

Another Royal Marine attack, backed by eight other Shermans, managed to penetrate the village. The SS, with few forces available, and threatened on the flank and from behind, pulled back under fire from five Shermans, to the town center

Fighting raged throughout the night. At dawn on June 12, the survivors reached the outposts west of Franqueville. The Divisionbegleitkompanie had held its positions with great sacrifice and withdrew a kilometer southwest of Rots.

Reinforcements Arrive

After a week of hard fighting, 12.SS-Pz.Div. Hitlerjugend had succeeded in blocking the Allied advance on the outskirts of Caen. The Allies had not been thrown back into the sea, but given the disproportion of the forces in the field, the young fighters of the Waffen-SS had still fought well despite the fact that most of them were experiencing their baptism of fire. Caen had been Montgomery's target for the attacks of June 7/8, but the city remained firmly in German hands. Caen, however, led to one important result: convincing the Führer that Normandy was the main Allied thrust, which resulted in the transfer of fresh troops to Normandy, such as the Leibstandarte from its bases in Belgium and Paul Hausser's II.SS-Panzerkorps, recalled from the Eastern Front.

SS-Ostuf. Michael Wittmann's 2.Kompanie of on the move to the Normandy front, June 7, 1944.

Schwere SS-Panzer-Abteilung 101, the independent heavy armored battalion assigned to I.SS-Pz.Korps, had started moving to the French front during the night of June 6/7, but it was only after five days' march that the Tigers reached Falaise, where they linked up with the Hitlerjugend.

SS-Hstuf. Möbius and his 1.Kompanie reached the area south of Caen on June 12. During the night, Möbius moved again, 10 kilometers northeast of Villers-Bocage, directly on the N175 that connected Caen with Villers-Bocage. Mobius had eight Tigers at his disposal. SS-Ostuf. Michael Wittmann's 2.Kompanie positioned on the left flank of the I.SS-Pz.Korps the same day. Wittmann had only six Tigers at his disposal; all the others had been damaged along the way, either due to Allied air attacks or mechanical problems. The Tigers had just been parked and camouflaged among the vegetation when a devastating Allied artillery bombardment began. Wittmann ordered an immediate change of position to limit losses. But the bombardment continued incessantly, following the Tigers. Wittmann was then forced to shift his positions for the third time, this time near Montbrocq hill, south of the N175.

Operation *Perch*

With the British and Canadian units stalled in front of Caen by the Hitlerjugend, Montgomery decided to attempt a breakthrough on the German left flank, which was the most exposed. The Panzer-Lehr Division had reinforced the Hitlerjugend defensive front, but their left flank was exposed and the Germans were unable to reestablish a continuous front between Caen and units fighting in western Normandy. Montgomery's response was Operation *Perch*: the British 7th Armoured Division was to move south and penetrate the left flank of the division, bypass its positions and pass through the village of Villers-Bocage, then advance on Caen, trapping both the Panzer-Lehr Division and the Hitlerjugend. On paper the plan looked perfect, but its execution turned out to be a disaster: the famous "Desert Rats," the 7th Armoured Division, suffered a significant defeat, inflicted by a single, determined Tiger commander. Clearly outnumbered, Wittmann, with six Tigers, prepared to do battle at Villers-Bocage.

The Battle of Villers-Bocage

In the early afternoon of June 12, 1944, Operation *Perch* opened, with Brigadier William "Loony" Hinde's 22nd Armoured Brigade in the van. Everything seemed to be going well until a single German antitank piece struck and knocked out a British Stuart tank near the village of Livery. Perhaps spooked, the British commander, Major-General Bobby Erskine, decided to stop for the night.

At dawn on June 13, the 7th Armoured Division combat group, under the command of the 22nd Armoured Brigade, moved on Villers-Bocage, with the order of march: 8th King's Royal Irish Hussars (a reconnaissance battalion), 4th County of London Yeomanry "Sharpshooters" (a tank battalion), 5th Royal Horse Artillery, 1/7 Queen's Royal Regiment (a battalion of infantry), 1st Battalion The Rifle Brigade (an armored infantry battalion, minus two companies), and the 26th Antitank battery.

The British met no resistance as they came into Villers-Bocage. The first to enter the town were the Cromwell tanks of the 4th County of London Yeomanry (4CLY), which undoubtedly revealed to the German command the enemy objectives: Villers-Bocage and the nearby Hill 213 alongside the main road leading to Caen. All of this was in the general framework of circumventing and annihilating the Hitlerjugend with a pincer maneuver.

Wittmann had left with his Tiger on reconnaissance in the direction of Villers-Bocage. Of its six available Tigers, Tiger 233 had a damaged track and SS-Ostuf. Wessel had been sent to make contact with a nearby unit to receive orders. Wittmann:

> I was in my command post and hadn't considered that the enemy might suddenly appear. I had sent one of my officers to make contact with a front-line unit and was waiting for him to return with news. Suddenly a soldier entered my command post and shouted: "Enemy tanks approaching." I immediately went outside and saw the enemy tanks about 150–200 meters away. At the same time, I saw that the tanks were accompanied by troop transport vehicles.

What Wittmann was seeing were the 4CLY tanks, which, after passing through Villers-Bocage, would move towards Hill 213 and then cut across to Caen. Of course, Wittmann was unaware of the general situation and had only a vague idea of what was afoot. Almost fascinated, he watched the terrible column of Cromwells and Shermans, accompanied by Bren carriers, traveling undisturbed along the national road towards Caen. "It was a whole armored regiment. This armored regiment really took me by surprise," he said later. One 4CLY squadron stopped on a hill east of the city on a tea break. Watching the British "bivouac" from the nearby forest where he was hiding, about 150 meters from Hill 213, Wittmann was amazed. When his gunner Bobby Woll said: "It seems they have already won the war!" to which Wittmann replied: "Let's show them that they are wrong!"

Wittmann knew well that this powerful Allied armored formation would not encounter any resistance before Caen. So, he decided to attack the entire enemy armored brigade alone, with his Tiger, even though he was aware it was a suicide mission: "Yes, I knew very well that that decision was senseless. Never as on that occasion, I was so impressed by the strength of the enemy, seeing those tanks advancing. But I knew I absolutely had to do it and I decided to hurl myself against the enemy."

Michael Wittmann.

Hitlerjugend Panther in Normandy. (NARA)

Hitlerjugend grenadiers during a lull in the fighting. (Michael Cremin collection)

SS-Stubaf. Krause, with his back to the left, consults the map.

Hitlerjugend gunners take cover in their position during an Allied assault.

A Hitlerjugend forward observer scans Allied positions with binoculars, hidden behind a destroyed Sherman tank.

Patry, abandoned by the Germans, also fell. On the night of June 16/17, Les Hauts Vents fell too.

On June 18, Allied attacks continued, investing III./26 north of the Parc de Boislande. At 1500, SS positions were subjected to a massive bombardment by Allied artillery. As the artillery began to lengthen its range, waves of tanks attacked, followed by infantry. Desperate hand-to-hand fighting ensued and despite the fierce resistance offered by the SS grenadiers, Allied units managed to advance to the southern side of the forests north of the park. Here, however, they came under fire from German artillery.

Toward sunset, III./26 launched a counterattack supported by tanks. Despite initial success, a massive artillery barrage stopped the Germans. When the counterattack failed, divisional HQ asked SS-Stubaf. Olboeter to recapture the Parc de Boislande. After a brief preparatory barrage by artillery and mortars, on June 18, Olboeter began a counterattack, moving from north of Fontenay, west of the road to Cristot. The *Panzergrenadieren* penetrated the park's forests, where bitter close-quarter fighting took place; some grenadiers managed to reach the northern edge of the park, but a heavy Allied artillery barrage prevented the arrival of reinforcements.

At the same time, the 7th Battalion Duke of Wellington with other armored units attacked and captured Hill 102. German counterattacks proved ineffectual. Also, on June 18, the 50th Division attacked Saint-Pierre and Tilly, occupying them. The Pz.-Lehr-Division unsuccessfully attempted to retake Tilly, after which the entire division assumed positions south and southwest of Montilly and Sagy. From Saint-Pierre, the Allies could now strike the left flank of III./26.

STADT DER AUSLANDSDEUTSCHEN
Nr. 25   21. Juni 1944   20 Pfg.

Stuttgarter Jllustrierte

INVASION!
Die deutschen Gegenmaßnahmen laufen!

The cover of a contemporary magazine: in the foreground is SS-Grenadier Otto Funk of 15./25 on a street in Rots.

East of the River Orne

Despite heavy fighting on the Hitlerjugend left flank, the Allies did not attack in the sector defended by SS-Pz.Gr.Rgt.25 apart from some localized actions. As early as June 13, the 51st (Highland) Division had begun to attack east of the River Orne against positions held by 21.Pz.Div., but with no success. Indeed, on June 16, it was troops of 21.Pz.Div. that attacked east of the Orne and reduced the British bridgehead, reoccupying Hérouvillette. The attack stopped in front of Escoville, where Allied resistance was particularly strong.

On June 18, the Divisionbegleitkompanie of the 12.SS was ordered to launch a counterattack to eliminate enemy advances in the Pz.Aufkl.Abt.130 sector; this action was successfully carried out by a *Schützen-Zug*, a rifle platoon, under SS-Ustuf. Erwin Stier and an *Infanterie-Geschütz-Zug* (infantry gun platoon). The main line of defense was restored and 120 prisoners were taken, including numerous officers. Success earned Stier the Iron Cross First Class. The Divisionbegleitkompanie remained in the Hottot area until June 20. The second battle for Caen ended with a clear defensive success for the Germans. Hitlerjugend losses up until June 16 were 403 dead, 847 wounded, and 63 missing. The vehicle inventory listed 52 PzKpfw IVs, 38 Panthers, 10 Wespes, and five Hummels.

An 8./SS-Pz.Rgt.12 PzKpfw IV recovered by the British.

| The Third Battle for Caen

On the defensive since June 10, the German forces in Normandy continued to resist the continuous Allied assaults, both in the east and in the west. On June 19, with the sudden deterioration of weather conditions across the Channel, there was a notable slowdown in the influx of Allied supplies and troops.

This unexpected event forced Montgomery to postpone Operation *Epsom* to the last week of June. Meanwhile, Rommel had received orders from Hitler to prepare a large counterattack against the Allied beachhead, attacking at the point of contact between the British and American forces, and then heading toward Bayeux with six armored divisions: I.SS-Pz. Korps of the II.SS-Pz.Korps, 21.Pz.Div., and the Pz.-Lehr-Div., but not all were immediately available. On June 24, the German high command held an orders group at the Panzergruppe West headquarters to discuss the final details of the counteroffensive, but the next day, the Allies attacked first.

Preliminary Attacks

The objective of the Allied offensive was another attempt to circumvent Caen from the west, using General O'Connor's VIII British Corps to drive a wedge between the Hitlerjugend and the Pz.-Lehr-Div., then continue eastward, cross the Odon River and take Hill 112, which dominated the whole area west of Caen.

Hitlerjugend grenadiers advancing in an open field during a counterattack.

A reconnaissance armored car in Normandy. (NARA)

After a massive preparatory artillery bombardment, Allied forces began their attack at 0500 but a thick fog prevented troops, defenders and attackers alike, from having a clear view of the situation. Many Allied units were scattered, losing contact with each other. Elements of the Hallamshire Battalion, of the 49th Inf.Div., which were to take western Fontenay, got completely lost and tried to cross the Fontenay–Tilly road but clashed with I./Pz.Gr. Lehr.Rgt.901. The rest of the Hallamshires crossed Bordel ridge but came under fire on the Fontenay–Juvigny road and stalled, taking heavy casualties.

It was a similar scenario with the 1/4 Battalion King's Own Yorkshire Light Infantry (146th Brigade) and the 11th Battalion Royal Scots Fusiliers (147th Brigade) which attacked west of the Hallams but got lost in the fog. When it cleared, the SS-Pz.Gr.Rgt.26, with artillery support, counterattacked along the Caen–Tilly road. The British suffered heavy casualties in bloody close-quarter combat.

In the southern Fontenay sector, SS grenadiers, well entrenched among the houses, desperately held the line. With the 146th Brigade penetrating a sector of the Pz.-Lehr-Div., and occupying the northern Tessel woods, the situation was only restored when SS-Stubaf. Olboeter led his last reserves in a counterattack, supported by tanks and artillery.

The 147th Brigade withdrew its 7th Battalion Duke of Wellington's Regiment and ordered it to attack the right flank of Olboeter's battalion. This fresh attack put III./26 in serious trouble, considering that they had lost contact with the divisional CP at Verson and Pz.Gr.Lehr-Rgt.901 had been breached. This opened up a dangerous gap for the Allies to push south to Noyers and Villers-Bocage. The Hitlerjugend was order to close it.

Under SS-Ostubaf. Max Wünsche, the Hitlerjugend launched the counterattack in the early afternoon, from the Tessel–Bretteville area in the direction of Fontaine. The leading platoon was, at his own request, led by SS-Ustuf. Heinz Schröder. The SS panzers came under enemy fire and Schröder's tank was hit at close range, with Schröder killed. Despite this initial hitch, the advance continued to the Fontenay–Juvigny road and contact with III./26 was established. However, contact with t the Pz.-Lehr-Division in Juvigny failed.

The Duke of Wellington then attacked III./26's right sector around 2100. The British had control of eastern Fontenay, except for some positions that remained firmly in German hands. The young SS grenadiers, assisted by artillery and panzers, fought like lions in the streets and houses of the village, contesting every inch of ground and inflicting heavy losses on the enemy, but they could not hold out for much longer. The situation also remained fragile on the left, where the Pz.-Lehr-Div. was stuck without any reserves.

At the same time, orders were issued for the main defensive line to be moved south of the Fontenay–Juvigny road. Fontenay was abandoned as the Hitlerjugend reinforced positions along the Saint-Martin–Tessel–Bretteville–Vendes line. The Tessel woods were in the hands of the Allies, a force estimated at an infantry battalion and 20 tanks. The Hitlerjugend HQ expected the enemy to continue its attack to the south on June 26, to widen the breach already opened between the German defenses.

Hitlerjugend grenadiers and a Panther in action in a village. (NARA)

In Profile:
PzKpfw IV Ausf. H of
12th SS-Pz.Div. Hitlerjugend

Technical specifications

PzKpfwIV Ausf H

Crew: 6
Weight: 25,000kg (27.58 tons)
Engine: TRM Maybach HL 120 12 cylinder, 300hp

Dimensions:
- Length (with gun forward) 7.2m (23'7")
- Length 5.89m (19'3")
- Width 3.29m (10'9")
- Height 2.68m (8'9")

Performance:
- Maximum speed (on road): 38 km/h (23 mph)
- Range (on road): 200km (124 miles)
- Ford: 1m (3'1"); slope: 60%; step: 0.6m (2');
  trench: 2.2m (7'2")

One of the best German tanks produced, the PzKpfw IV was the backbone of the German Panzerdivisionen. The first version entered production in 1934 as the PzKpfw IV Ausf A, or SdKfz 161. It mounted a short 7.5cm gun, a 7.92mm coaxial machine gun and another machine gun of the same caliber on the frontal glacis. Maximum armor thickness was 20mm in the turret and 14.5mm in the hull. Only a few models were produced in the 1936/7 period. The next model, the PzKpfw IV Ausf B, had thicker armor, a more powerful engine and other improvements. Throughout the long period during which the PzKpfw IV remained in production, the basic hull remained unchanged; nevertheless, to face the growing threat of enemy anti-tank weapons, armor thickness was increased and new weapons were installed. Various versions were produced, up to J, over the course of the war; the definitive production model, the PzKpfw IV Ausf J, made its appearance in March 1944. Main armament consisted of a long-barrelled 7.5cm gun that used a wide range of ammunition, including smoke and high-explosive rounds. Hitlerjugend was mainly supplied with H and later versions.

I.SS-Pz.Korps ordered Hitlerjugend and the Pz-Lehr-Div. to counterattack on June 26, to establish a new defensive line. However, the Hitlerjugend complained of insufficient armor to do so; a promise of Tiger tanks had failed to materialize. In the meantime, Operation *Epsom* was about to break.

Operation *Epsom*

During the night of June 25/26, Wünsche assembled his troops for the counterattack. It was still dark when SS-Staf. Kurt Meyer left his CP to move to Rauray. The whole front appeared calm, radio surveillance had not detected anything in particular; however, the high command were convinced that a large-scale operation was imminent. The barrage that had preceded the 49th Division attack on Fontenay the day before signified more than a localized assault. And so it was that the Kampfgruppe Wünsche attack from Rauray and the British attack from the Tessel forest ran into each other at dawn.

The Hitlerjugend armored attack initially progressed well, but stalled with the simultaneous enemy attack, SS-Ustuf. Rolf Jauch, an officer in I./SS-Pz.Rgt.12, reported:

> The attack stopped and we found ourselves under enemy fire from three sides.
> My Panther's cannon failed—the pinion gear was defective—and I went with my

SS-Ostubaf. Max Wünsche congratulates one of his men who distinguished himself in combat. In the background is SS-Hstuf. Schlauss, communications officer in SS-Pz.Rgt.12.

A PzKpfw IV of II./SS-Pz.Rgt.12 on the march.

gunner to retrieve one from a damaged panzer abandoned on the eastern side of the valley. On the way back we ended up under enemy fire from the right sector. My gunner, Gumspert, was killed and I was hit in the elbow and grazed in the chest. I managed to bring the pinion gear and put my panzer back in order. Jürgensen [the commander of the *Abteilung*] ordered me to move east and from there south since it was impossible to have me moved to an aid station in an ambulance.

Kurt Meyer:

The day was about to begin. Everything was still calm. I was near Rauray with Max Wünsche and I watched the last of our panzers start for the assembly area. The German batteries began their barrage. A British air attack, with low-flying aircraft, developed soon after, with rockets hitting the entire Rauray sector. The hell of battle had begun, with the first tanks moving toward the front. The attack initially progressed well, but was soon stopped by a British counterattack and turned into a battle between tanks, which fought with great determination. The uneven terrain, covered by hedges, did not allow our panzers to take advantage of the increased range of their guns. In particular, the lack of infantry was a factor. The concentration of artillery fire limited any possible cooperation and subsequently also made it impossible to give direct commands. There were no sounds of battle from the area east of Rauray. All the fighting was concentrated farther west … It started to rain. Thank God; this would protect us from enemy fighter-bombers. But suddenly, the ground seemed to open up as if to devour us all. Within seconds, all hell broke loose. Rauray turned into a mass of rubble and uprooted trees. I found myself lying in a canal along the road, stunned by the roar of the ongoing battle … Fog joined the gases of the explosions. I still couldn't understand the situation on the ground, all contact was disrupted. Was this perhaps the great enemy offensive we were waiting for?

The divisional commander ordered Wünsche to stop the enemy attack immediately and hold Rauray at all costs, before returning to his CP at Verson.

Tiger "222" of 2.Kompanie in the shelter of trees.

At 0730 on June 26, Allied artillery began preparatory fire, hitting German positions on the VIII Corps attack front: the barrage concentrated on the front lines for 10 minutes, then rolled forward progressively at three-minute intervals. The 7th Royal Tank attacked with the Cameronians (9th Battalion) near Le Mesnil, but ended up in the minefields established by Hitlerjugend pioneers, to the southeast and southwest of the village, and lost 10 tanks. The British infantry was forced to continue its advance with little armored support. SS-Pz.Gr.Rgt.26's antitank guns opened fire from the area south of Fontanay II./SS-Art.Rgt.12 and the Flak pieces of Flaksturmregiment 4 also concentrated their fire on the approaching enemy infantry.

At around 1100, the Glasgow Highlanders reached the northern part of Cheux. The Cameronians were on the right, with their tanks pinned farther back by well-camouflaged German antitank guns. Around noon, the 11th Armoured Division moved to the area north of Cheux but its forward elements also ended up in a minefield, while other tanks pushed through the ruins of the village, where they were attacked by SS grenadiers at close range with hand grenades and Panzerfausts. Allied tanks reached the southern part of Cheux around 1300. But their recon patrols were annihilated by tank fire from the southwest and southeast. Other Allied units reached Grainville around 1500. Another massive Allied artillery bombardment resulted in significant German losses. Positions held by Hitlerjugend pioneers appeared tenuous, as reported by SS-Ustuf. Hans Richter:

> The enemy's barrage focused on the positions of SS-Pz.Pi.Btl.12 and on the command post, starting at 0245. The night was clear. No enemy activity was reported. The barrage resumed at 0600. At 0615, the commander, SS-Stubaf. Siegfried Müller, spotted a concentration of tanks in the southern part of Le Mesnil-Patry with his binoculars. He immediately requested artillery support …

In Profile:
Obersturmbannführer Max Wünsche

Max Wünsche was born on April 20, 1914, in Kittlitz (Löbau). He joined the SS in July 1933 before promotion to *Untersturmführer* in the Leibstandarte SS-Adolf Hitler (LSSAH) in 1935. After a spell providing personal security to Hitler, he returned to LSSAH for the invasion of the Low Countries and France, serving under Kurt Meyer. During Operation *Marita*, the invasion of the Balkans, and *Barbarossa*, the invasion of the Soviet Union, he served as adjutant to Sepp Dietrich. In February 1942, Wünsche assumed command of the LSSAH Sturmgeschütz battalion, which served with distinction during the 1943 battles of Kharkov. In one action alone, his unit destroyed 47 artillery pieces and antitank guns. In June 1943, he joined the new Hitlerjugend division. In Normandy, he saw continuous action from June 7 to August 20, when he was captured by British troops while trying to escape the Falaise Pocket. He spent the rest of the war as a PoW in Scotland before his release in 1948. He died in Munich, aged 80, on April 17, 1995. He held the Iron Cross (1st and 2nd Class), the German Cross in Gold, and the Knight's Cross of the Iron Cross with Oak Leaves.

SS-Stubaf. Max Wünsche. (BDC)

Wünsche aboard a Panther. (NARA)

At around 0700, SS-Obersturmführer Bischoff reported that the unit on his left had pulled back 200–300 meters during the night and that his left flank was therefore exposed. This was immediately reported to the divisional command. Also at 0700, contact with 2.Kompanie was lost. Enemy tanks were slowly advancing against the positions on the left and those of the battalion. The commander requested the support of the panzers and reported the matter to the commander of SS-Pz.Gr.Rgt.26. However, contact with this regiment had been cut and so he sent his aide to alert the panzers grouped behind our sector to counterattack, but by 0815, the panzers had not yet arrived. The commander sent two runners in quick succession to get the tanks into position. Suddenly, enemy machine-gun fire fell upon us and in a short time, clouds of smoke and dust obscured our visibility. At around 0830, the commander of Pi.Erk.-Zug [scout platoon], SS-Oberscharführer Vogel, came to report. He was wounded and reported that enemy tanks had been sighted on the Fontenay-le-Pesnel–Carpiquet road. Vogel was ordered to defend the CP. At 0900, SS-Unterscharführer Hemken spotted approaching enemy tanks. The commander jumped out of his bunker and saw in turn, left and right, enemy tanks, armored cars and infantry advancing in the direction of Cheux. He immediately ordered "open fire" on the Allied infantry. The enemy for his part attacked the bunker and trenches with tanks, firing with cannons and machine guns. The men retreated, fighting towards the bunker. The last soldier managed to enter the bunker as an enemy tank fired into it three times. Hand grenades were thrown, which filled the bunker with smoke and dust. Some soldiers were slightly wounded by the shrapnel from the grenades. It was a real miracle.

Scottish soldiers of the 15th Scottish Division with Hitlerjugend prisoners belonging to II./26 and I./SS-Pz.Art.Rgt.12 captured in the Haut du Bosq area on June 26, 1944.

Aid to a lightly wounded grenadier.

Saint-Manvieu

At the same time, the 44th Brigade, together with the 9th Royal Tank, launched its attack, having as its objective the villages of La Gaule and Saint-Manvieu. The 6th Royal Scots Fusiliers reached the northern suburbs of Saint-Manvieu and throughout the morning clashes erupted in streets and houses. From the VIII Corps diary:

> Two houses in particular were defended with great determination and were eventually cleaned out with flamethrowers. The 8th Royal Scots reached La Gaule at around 0830. Again, breakthrough into the village was only possible after hard fighting. By 1130, both battalions had reached the southern suburbs of the two villages. It seemed that these positions were firmly in our hands, but numerous hotbeds of resistance were still active and still required fighting. This, along with a number of counterattacks, made the situation more difficult than we expected!

SS-Unterscharführer Heinrich Bassenauer, of the 4./26 Granatwerferzug (mortar platoon), reported:

> Three of our mortars had already been lost due to direct enemy fire and many of the comrades of our platoon were killed or wounded. The enemy had come up to the trees and hedges near our position. We were also surrounded by tanks that were aiming their guns at us from a distance. With the remaining two mortars, we decided to fall back towards the battalion command post, taking up positions among the granaries, to remain well hidden from the enemy. We had to return several times to our previous positions, to recover ammunition for our mortars, suffering new losses due to enemy fire. Our own barrage fire prevented the enemy infantry from advancing further. When a British flamethrower tank pushed up to the entrance of the battalion command post, it was as if all of a sudden everything

A Hitlerjugend gunner next to an s.IG 33 heavy infantry gun.

disintegrated … between roars and hisses the horizon turned red and black.

A 1./26 runner, SS-Sturmmann Aribert Kalke, described the clashes in Saint-Manvieu, near the battalion command post, located in a large house along the Rots–Cheux road:

The artillery fire was intensifying, eventually concentrating on the center of the village. The explosions reached the courtyard in front of us, near the entrance to the command post. The house was shaken by numerous rounds. Between the explosions, you could hear the brief, dull sound of gunfire from enemy tanks. The battalion staff was under cover in the basement. Only a few men remained on the upper floors. Radio links with the companies had been cut and the situation appeared increasingly confused. The commander of the battalion, SS-Stubaf. Krause, was just sending a courier to the 2.Kompanie when a messenger from this same company arrived. He was wounded and reported that the company commander, SS-Obersturmführer Siegfried Gröschel, and his aide were killed. The

Grenadiers and a Panther in the Rauray sector. (Münchner Illustrierte Press)

company had engaged in bitter hand-to-hand combat and had been completely overwhelmed. Some enemy tanks soon arrived in front of our command post. The commander ordered his aide to make contact with a *Panzerkompanie* in the Bijude area [2 kilometers southeast], to counterattack immediately. SS-Ustuf. Walter Hölzel took me with him as his runner. Another *Untersturmführer* on the battalion staff as liaison officer from the regiment joined us. When enemy artillery fire subsided slightly, we left the command post by a rear exit one at a time. A small wooded area behind the house served as cover. After climbing a small slope, we found ourselves in a cornfield, which continued to cover our movements. Right among the wheat, I lost sight of the two officers. When I crossed the Fontenay–Caen road, I found myself under rifle and machine-gun fire from the right. Totally lost, I passed through an aid station and shortly after, I found SS-Untersturmführer Hölzel and together we reached the *Panzerkompanie*. The commander however categorically refused to launch a counterattack without adequate infantry support. Without the infantry in tow, the panzers could not fight in the streets.

The Sacrifice of Emil Dürr

The hero of that day was undoubtedly SS-Unterscharführer Emil Dürr, *geschützführe* (gun chief) in the 4./26 Panzerabwehrzug (antitank defense platoon). An unknown war correspondent tells us of his action and his death:

> Increasingly harsh, the tank shells continued to hit the park. The beams of the house turned to splinters, while the bricks of the park wall began to fly in every direction. The earth was shaking. In the early hours of June 26, 1944, while the sun was still resting behind the Norman hills, the British barrage had begun. For at least three hours, they relentlessly struck the main defensive line in front of Saint-Manvieu and the village itself and on the grenadiers of I.Bataillon of a

Divisional Insignia

The divisional emblem was chosen following a competition organized in November 1943 and won by Franz Lang. The "cut" of the upper right part of the shield, served to specify that the unit was an armored division. The ornamental oak leaves were a reminder that the first divisional commander, SS-Obf. Witt, had been decorated with Oak Leaves. The other elements inside the shield had a double symbolic function: the victory rune (*Sig-Rune*), which was the emblem of the *Deutsches Jungvolk* in the Hitlerjugend (which grouped children between 10 and 14 years old), was a reference to the common origin of volunteers. The *Passepartout* (latchkey, or *Dietrich* in German), was a reference to the fact that the cadres of the division came mainly from the Leibstandarte.

The divisional emblem, painted in white.

regiment of the SS-Panzerdivision Hitlerjugend, who were awaiting a large-scale enemy offensive against the airport of Carpiquet and along the Orne River for days and hours in front of the gates of Caen. The foxholes were wiped out, the machine-gun emplacements were destroyed, and the men mercilessly torn to pieces. Ammunition stockpiles blew up, telephone poles collapsed, and torn electrical wires "screeched" in the streets. Houses caught fire, walls collapsed. The earth suffered its wounds, dug into the ground in infinite numbers.

When three hours later, the enemy guns fell silent with splinters still hissing in the air, the enemy tanks advanced through the smoke, stench, and fog. They penetrated the positions and hit Saint-Manvieu. Like a pack of hungry wolves, they surrounded the park. The handful of men defending the battalion command post counted at least 15 Shermans. They were positioned in front of the wall that protected one side of the park and in the cornfield on the other side. Anyone who could wield a weapon was thrown into battle, runners, clerks, etc. If they crossed the bridge in front of the grenadiers, if they pushed into the park, then it would be over. The already battered battalion would have lost the initiative and the course of the battle would have taken a bad turn. If the British breakthrough were to be successful, the enemy would have crossed the River Orne, using the last intact bridge near Saint-André, reached the Caen–Falaise road and attacked Caen from the south. The battalion's command post then became an important defensive bastion, but there were no heavy weapons. There were only machine guns and rifles, Panzerfausts, and magnetic charges. And just a handful of men.

These could have only minimal effect against a dozen tanks. A minimal effect? Who could tell? They had Unterscharführer Dürr with them. But no one could predict the outcome of that critical moment. Not even the young, blond *Unterscharführer* knew … But two mortars were still in the park, massive and

Emil Dürr. (BDC)

powerful. And their crew still had 25 rounds at their disposal. They fired at the tank … their grenades exploded with a crash, causing confusion. Some sharpshooters crept through the hedges and climbed the wall, to fire at the tank commanders, who had come out too early with their heads from their hatches. Some tanks turned back. They thought that the forces in the park were numerous and did not want to go through it. However, the calm did not last long: the tanks returned and began firing. They took the house as their target, damaging it to such an extent that it was necessary to evacuate the wounded from it. Then suddenly, a cry of alarm was raised among the troops holding the position. An enemy flamethrower tank had arrived at the park entrance, which dominated the road to the command post, about to hit it at any moment. "This tank

A Hitlerjugend 7.5cm PaK 40 antitank position.

must be stopped," the commander ordered. Unterscharführer Dürr had heard the order; he didn't hesitate. "I'm going," he said.

It was difficult to get close to the tank. It was positioned to dominate the ground around it from three sides. Unterscharführer Dürr climbed up the inner courtyard wall and moved towards the tank. But the round from the Panzerfaust failed to pierce the tank. Maybe he hadn't aimed carefully in the excitement of the moment. Then Dürr felt a blow in his chest and soon after a hot substance was dripping down his thighs. Angry, Dürr pulled himself up. He retrieved another Panzerfaust and moved toward the tank a second time. This time the distance was greater, so he aimed for the tracks. The tank stalled, a track tore off. But once again, Dürr was targeted by machine-gun fire. Though wounded, he scaled the wall, out of range of enemy fire. He spotted a magnetic mine and took possession of it. A comrade tried to bring him back: "You're losing blood." But enemy tank had to be stopped. For the third time he made the dangerous trip.

He climbed the wall. He ran, stumbling, toward the tank, paying no attention to the bullets. Now he was closer, one more jump, and he attached the charge. He was about to leave, when he heard a rumble behind him: the charge had fallen to the ground. And once again he moved to the flamethrower tank. He grabbed the charge and pushed it back against the tank. Then came the fire, the flames, the darkness before his eyes. When he fell to the ground, he saw the tank burning. He tried to get up, but he couldn't. He crept along the path, now open, that led to the command post. His comrades spotted him, picked him up and took him to a doctor. Four hours later he passed away. Not a word of regret escaped his lips. On his grave, the commander bestowed on him the Knight's Cross of the Iron Cross, the first NCO of the 12.SS-Panzer-Division to receive it.

Attrition

After the German counterattack was interrupted near Tessel–Bretteville, the two armored companies attempted to regain these two lost positions. SS-Ustuf. Willi Kändler, an officer at 5.Pz.Kp. noted:

> Numerous enemy tanks of various types were spotted on the hill to our left. They came from Le Mesnil and headed in the direction of Cheux. We were caught in a violent armored duel. A few meters in front of my panzer, SS-Untersturmführer Buchholz was in his turret. His panzer took a direct hit and the officer's head was severed. Meanwhile, a column of British tanks had already broken through, moving towards Cheux and so the company retreated southward, continuing to fight. We settled into new positions on both sides of Route Départemental No. 23 [from Noyers to Cheux]. The platoons of Ustuf. Karl Heinz Porsch and Ustuf. Helmut Kunze took up positions north of Hill 112. I went into position with the remaining four or five panzers of my platoon south of it, a little farther south, and along the way met some Shermans advancing southwest on a parallel track. At close range I destroyed five of these tanks.

By noon, the situation was as follows: the positions in the Saint-Manvieu sector east of Fontenay had been overwhelmed. Saint-Manvieu itself had been captured by the enemy with attacks from the north and southwest and only some positions were still resisting. 1. and 3.Kp., in position to the east and northeast of the village, behind the crest of Mue, near SS-Pz.Gr.Rgt.25 on the right, found themselves boxed in by the Scots. 9.Pz.Kp. (minus one platoon), in position behind the battalion sector, had managed to repel an armored attack against the Carpiquet airfield. Allied forces had pushed into Cheux with tanks and infantry. However, service units of the Pionier-Bataillon and SS-Pz.Gr.Rgt.26 were still holding out.

SS-Pz.Gren.Rgt.25 defensive position north of Caen.

SS-Pz.Gren.Rgt.25 grenadiers on a halftrack.

Due to the failure of their attacks on Rauray from Tessel, the Allies were unable to progress farther south. Allied armored units instead broke through southeast of Cheux, near the crossing over the Odon at Verson and south of Tourville.

Meanwhile, around noon, the Allies deployed the 29th Armoured Brigade (11th Armoured Division) to the north of Cheux. From here, it advanced on Gavrus with the 2nd Battalion Fife and Forfar Yeomanry (2FFY), an armored formation, and on Tourmanville, with the 23rd Hussars. 2FFY moved west of Cheux and was involved in clashes with elements of II./SS-Pz.Rgt.12, before passing through the village. The battle was confusing: the 23rd Hussars reached the center of the village, but were blocked by antitank guns and artillery. Eventually, both British armored formations were stalled in their advance by the ruins of the village itself and strong German resistance.

Along the Odon, Allied attacks were not long in coming: the 227th Infantry Brigade had orders to seize a river crossing: the 2nd Argyll and Sutherland Highlanders were to take the bridges at Gavrus and Tourmanville. Haut du Bosq had not been captured with SS Panzers and grenadiers dug in in small groups. British infantry advanced slowly, under a heavy barrage unleashed by the Hitlerjugend pioneers. It was impossible for the Allied tanks to negotiate the ruins of the village. The 10th Highland Light Infantry (HLI) was blocked by panzer fire as it attempted to move to the south of Haut du Bosq. The 2nd Gordon Highlanders, reinforced by a company of the 9th Royal Tanks, advanced to the left but was also blocked by panzers and machine guns as it approached Hill 100 south of Cheux. Some British tanks were destroyed and the infantry suffered heavy losses. The commander of the Gordons, after the withdrawal of the panzers, had his men withdraw to defensive positions south of Cheux.

Hitlerjugend panzer in Normandy. (Michael Cremin collection)

A New Defensive Line

Unable to reestablish the previous defensive line, the Hitlerjugend HQ, with Corps approval, established new defensive positions along the Marcelet hills south of the Cheux–Rauray–Vendes line. An attempt was made to relieve the surrounded CP at Saint-Manvieu but was blocked by enemy artillery fire. SS-Stubaf. Krause advised the CP to break out on their own that night, which they successfully did.

On the left wing of the division, where Kampfgruppe Wünsche was engaged, fighting continued throughout the day. The grenadiers of the III./26, together with the attached *Pionierzug*, repelled all attacks as well as managing to counterattack with the panzers of the 6. and 8.Pz.Kp. In the afternoon, Wünsche had to detach 8.Pz.Kp. in support of II./SS-Pz. Rgt.12, engaged in the Cheux area. Due to strong Allied pressure, the SS units subsequently withdrew to the north of Cheux. The new Hitlerjugend defensive line consisted, especially in the central sector, of a series of fortified points, which could, due to lack of forces, be easily bypassed. Fresh Allied attacks were expected for June 27, again from the area of Cheux, Saint-Manvieu, and Norrey, to capture Caen. At that time, the division's armored force numbered 30 PzKpfw IVs and 17 Panthers, in addition to other PzKpfw IVs and StuGs of the two attached companies of 21.Panzer-Division.

On the evening of June 26, SS-Brigdf. Krämer reported the situation to 7.Armee headquarters: "Enemy breakthroughs between Saint-Manvieu–Tessel–Bretteville to the south. Two hours ago, enemy vanguards arrived in Grainville. Our units are still stationed on both sides of Cheux. If no new reinforcements arrive in the night, a new breakthrough in the same area of Cheux cannot be avoided."

An hour later, around 2100, the commander of 7.Armee, Generaloberst Dollmann, discussed the situation with Rommel who suggested using II.SS-Pz.Korps in a counterattack, to prevent at all costs the Hitlerjugend and 21.Pz.Div. being surrounded. However, the counterattack came to naught.

Hitlerjugend artillery in Normandy. (Michael Cremin collection)

A Waffen-SS grenadier in Normandy. (DWS)

Leibstandarte grenadiers in action. The LSSAH fought alongside the Hitlerjugend for much of the Normandy campaign. (NARA)

Fresh Attacks by VIII Corps

At dawn on June 27, Allied units returned to attack with the aim of seizing the crossings on the Odon. However, when the 10HLI reached its assembly area before launching the attack on Gavrus, it found itself under fire from German machine guns and mortars, taking heavy casualties. Meanwhile, 17 2.Pz.Div. Panthers, instead of coordinating their action with other units, attacked on their own initiative in the direction of Cheux, reporting the loss of six tanks.

The few remaining German forces in the sector were left with the difficult task of preventing an Allied breakthrough into Noyers, which would have threatened the defenses south of Cheux and the right wing of the Pz-Lehr-Division. The Allied attack on Rauray began at 0800; the 11th Durham Light Infantry immediately fell under German fire, suffering heavy casualties. Only the intervention of Shermans forced the German defenders to retreat north of Brettevillette in the afternoon.

The 49th Division reported: "Today we captured Rauray, which was defended by the enemy with determination for at least two days. His infantry and tanks defended every inch of territory north and east of the city against all of. our attacks." To prevent the expansion of the breakthrough towards Verson and Grainville, a Panther company and PzKpfw IVs

A German antitank squad in a French village.

SS-Stubaf. Albert Frey. (BDC)

of 21.Pz.Div. were transferred to the front line west of Verson. Scattered German units in Grainville, south and southwest of Cheux and on both sides of Brettevillette conducted sporadic defensive operations.

In one clash the CO 5./SS-Pz. Rgt.12.,SS-Ostuf. Helmut Bando, was killed. SS-Ustuf. Willy Kändler, CO III.Zug of 5.Pz.Kp., recalled:

Once our panzers were on the front line, they found themselves under the intense and constant fire of antitank guns and enemy guns. I was wounded in the head by shrapnel from an antitank round. I remained in position, but my gunner Koloska, who was badly wounded, had to be evacuated. At about 1100, my company commander, Bando, came up close to my panzer. He pointed to an enemy machine gun to the right of a farm that

SS-Stubaf. Gerd Bremer. (BDC)

was shooting at us, and ordered me to attack it. As he turned to leave, a burst from that same machine gun hit him in the back of the head, killing him.

The priority at that time was to stabilize the front and reestablish its continuity before any new Allied attacks occurred. Fresh troops were therefore committed to the theater. Elements of 1.SS-Pz.Div. LSSAH arrived from Belgium and, at Rommel's behest, Kampfgruppe Weidinger of the Das Reich was engaged in the Grainville area.

Fighting on June 28

Also on June 28, Allied and Germans plans collided: VIII Corps attempted to expand its bridgehead to the south and west. Hitlerjugend, for its part, was committed to preventing the Allies from capturing Hill 112 and forcing a crossing of the Orne. Thanks to the reinforcement of the Weidinger's *Kampfgruppe*, a new counterattack from Verson to the west was also planned to cut off British forces on the same bridgehead. However, despite being subjected to an artillery bombardment, tanks of the 23rd Hussars managed to advance up to the foot of Hill 112 where they came under fire from the panzers of Pz.Rgt.12, deployed south of Fontaine-Etoupefour and in the wooded area northeast of Baron. By 12 noon, however, they had occupied the northern part of the hill and were soon reinforced by the 3rd Royal Tank.

Kampfgruppe Weidinger then took control of the Mondrainville–Tessel–Bretteville sector, while a Panther company defended the eastern slopes of Hill 113, 2 kilometers west of Esquay, farther north. As reported by SS-Oscha. Willy Kretschmar, 5.Pz.Kp. arrived in

Esquay around 0800. Two hours later, II./SS-Pz.Rgt.12 under SS-Stubaf. Prinz attacked Hill 112 from the southeast and south.

Kretschmar described the attack:

> After regrouping quickly, we began the attack in a spread-out formation, at 0930 or 1000. We pushed forward, each Panther covering the other. Without precise targets, we fired antitank and explosive rounds into the forest. The move went quickly. About 300 to 400 meters from the forest, we spotted some British soldiers moving among the trees. We fired our machine guns. About a 100 meters from the forest, we changed the order of formation, to a narrower front, as between the trees there was a passage between 80 and 100 meters wide. The slope on our left was covered with bushes and trees. In the meantime, I had taken the lead with my panzer. We were moving in a northwest direction. The cannon was positioned at 12 o'clock and an antitank round was ready in the barrel. Behind me, the panzer of SS-Uscha. Jürgens was moving forward.

SS-Stubaf.
Otto Weidinger.
(BDC)

SS-Uscha. Gerhard Mahlke's Panther "438." (NARA)

His cannon was positioned at 3 o'clock, in the direction of the forest so that he would not be surprised by an enemy bazooka. At the edge of the forest, I ordered a stop to examine the terrain. I scanned the area to the right in front of us with my binoculars to spot enemy tanks and antitank pieces. But I saw nothing suspicious. Then I ordered the advance o resume. After traveling a few meters, there was a sudden explosion: we were hit by a shot coming from the right, direction 3 o'clock. I ordered the driver, Sturmmann Schneider: "Go back!" He reacted immediately, turned the tank around and went into cover at great speed. At that point, the forest seemed to come alive, rifle and machine gun-fire began hitting our tank, but at the same time we received fire support from some of our mortars and artillery. We returned to our former staging area without any casualties. There, we inspected our tank to assess the damage.

A new attack with II./SS-Pz.Rgt.12 panzers was planned for the afternoon. Meanwhile, around noon, four 6.Pz.Kp panzers under Standartenoberjunker Kurt Muhlhaus, went to reconnoiter Hill 112 from the southeast.

The Attack of the Leibstandarte

Also on June 28, LSSAH SS-Pz.Gr.Rgt.1, with Weidinge's *Kampfgruppe*, was ordered to counterattack west from Verson on both sides of the Caen–Villers-Bocage road and advance on Mondrainville to cut off Allied forces that had crossed the Odon. Pz.Rgt.22 with PzKpfw Ivs, SS-Pz.Rgt.12 with Panthers, and SS-Pz.Abt.101. with Tigers, III./SS-Art.Rgt.12 and the Werfer Abteilung were to provide support fire. The attack began at 0600, after assembly west of Verson. The *Panzergrenadieren* of the Waffen-SS, supported by panzers, seized the northern part of Mouen occupied by the Monmouthshires.

Allied units attempted to retreat along the railway line after suffering heavy losses. Part of SS-Pz.Gr.Rgt.1 continued to Colleville, where in the afternoon, the SS troops blocked the advance of 10HLI towards Mouen. After the intervention of the artillery, the HLI launched its attack, supported by the tanks of the 3rd Battalion The City of London Yeomanry, but the Germans managed to repel it nonetheless. Late in the evening, the British brought in two further armored formations, with which they finally took Mouen, forcing the SS units to retreat after suffering serious losses. However, the 70th Infantry Brigade's attack in the Brettevillette sector was repulsed.

Following the failure to widen the bridgehead, together with the German counterattacks and the arrival of II.SS-Pz.Korps, the Allies suspended their offensive. Despite overwhelming superiority, the British had overestimated the size of the German forces and in particular that of the Hitlerjugend.

A Hitlerjugend Sig-33 heavy infantry gun. (Michael Cremin collection)

New Orders

On the same day, June 28, Panzergruppe West issued fresh orders for the forces engaged in Normandy, which can be summarized as:

- Defend current positions.
- Prepare for a concentrated counterattack to destroy American forces in the Balleroy area, as well as enemy forces east of the Orne River.
- Prepare for a counterattack to eliminate possible enemy breakthroughs, from the Caen area and west of it.

Panzergruppe West intended to attack beyond the Gavrus–Noyers line on June 29, with Hausser's II.SS-Pz-Korps, to take Baron, Mouen, Cheux and destroy enemy forces that had crossed the Caen–Villers-Bocage road. But already on the evening of June 28, Generaloberst Dollmann, commander of 7.Armee, decided that the situation on the Hitlerjugend front was so precarious as to order SS-Obstgruf. Hausser to launch an immediate counterattack against the western flank of the British salient. Hausser replied that his troops needed at least another day of rest. Dollmann found himself in trouble, considering that he was already under investigation for the loss of Cherbourg two days earlier. He committed suicide. Consequently, Hausser replaced him in command of 7.Armee.

The business end of a Jagdpanzer IV.

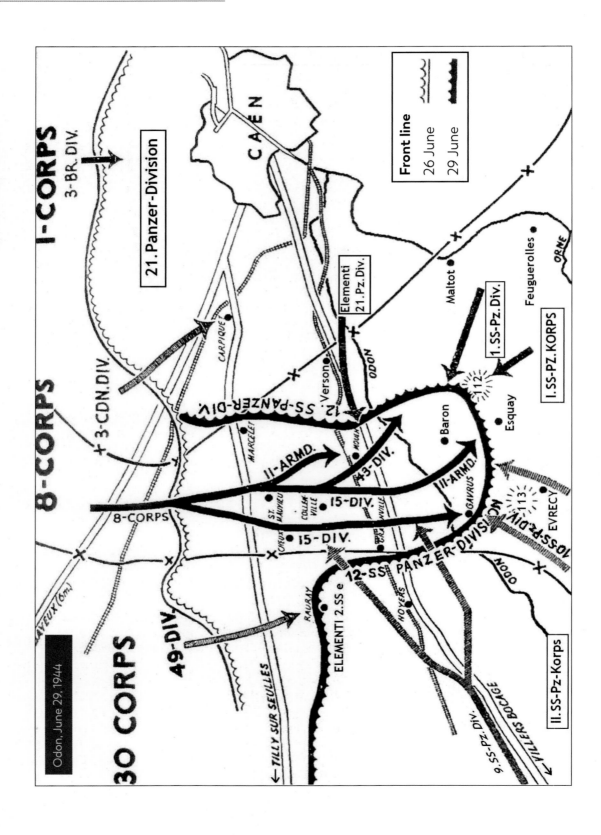

German Jagdpanzer IV in Normandy.

Counteroffensive of June 29

The deployment and grouping of II.SS-Pz.Korps units continued throughout the night and the early hours of June 29. The start of the attack, set for 0600, had to be postponed to 1400 due to delays in the assembly of the SS units.

But it was the British who attacked first: the 8th Royal Scots and 6th Royal Scots Fusiliers reached the railway embankment west of Grainville at around 1040. The 2nd Gordons in Tourville and the HLI at Colleville, were replaced by troops of the 214th Brigade, who subsequently regrouped south of Mondrainville to advance on Gavrus. The Worcesters of the 43rd Division attacked Mouen and secured control of it around 1100. The 129th Infantry Brigade instead attacked from south of Mouen, in the direction of Baron, taking the village at 1830. The 159th Infantry Brigade reinforced the bridgehead at Tourmanville, harassed only by German mortar fire. At noon, the 29th Armoured Brigade made a fresh attempt to take Hill 112 and Esquay.

From the first light of dawn, the 40th Royal Tanks had tried to bypass the German positions in Esquay, without success. The 8th Battalion Rifle Brigade, backed by the 3rd Royal Tanks, attacked the wooded area 300 meters east of Hill 112—the *Kastenwaldchen*, the small square forest. Only a few Hitlerjugend panzers retaliated. At the same time, the 2nd Fife and Forfar Yeomanry moved to the left, intending to support the attack, but was blocked by fire from the Château de Fontaine area. Around 1100, SS-Pz.Rgt.12 had to fall back as the enemy now occupied the *Kastenwaldchen*. In response, German artillery and mortars struck the position throughout the day. At the same time, tanks from the 3rd Battalion Royal Tank Regiment attacked from the northwest of Hill 112, moving south and southwest. On their way they encountered six Tigers which confronted them and annihilated them completely.

A Waffen-SS MG 42 team in action, Normandy, 1944. (NARA)

Panzergruppe West's daily report regarding the battle on Hill 112 reported: "An enemy column composed of about 50 tanks and infantry troops, moving from Baron in the direction of Château de Fontaine was destroyed by the fire of our artillery and our mortars." Also according to the daily report, the II.SS-Pz.Korps attack started at 1430. 9.SS-Pz.Div. attacked on both sides of the Noyers–Cheux road, with SS-Pz.Gr.Rgt.20 on the right, SS-Pz. Gr.Rgt.19 in the center, and Kampfgruppe Weidinger on the left. SS-Pz.Rgt.9 supported the attack. The SS units managed to break through between Valtru, held by the 7th Seaforths, and Grainville, held by 9th Cameronians. However, the breach was immediately closed with the intervention of the 9th Royal Tanks and above all with the barrage unleashed by Allied artillery and air forces. By around 1800, the Allies had recovered all the lost positions. Farther north, along the railway embankment near Grainville, a Hohenstaufen attack overwhelmed two companies of the 8th Royal Scots.

However, even this success was quickly negated by the arrival numerous Allied forces. At around 1400, panzers managed to probe as far as Cheux, but were soon stopped and destroyed by Allied fire. In the afternoon, the Hohenstaufen attack was definitively blocked by an enemy barrage: the SS units were forced to fall back on their start positions, with considerable losses. South of the Odon, the Frundsberg, with SS-Pz.Gr.Rgt.21, took Evrecy and Hill 113. An attempt to continue to Esquay was however blocked. On the left, SS-Pz. Gr.Rgt.22, also supported by panzers and pioneers, took Gavrus. A British counterattack repelled the SS units south and southwest of the city a few hours later.

During the evening, VIII Corps received the order from Second Army to stop any further attack in the direction of the Orne River and consolidate the gains. For their part, I. and II.SS-Pz.Korps, postponed further attacks to regroup.

Hitlerjugend grenadier advancing with an MG 42. (Michael Cremin collection)

The Counteroffensive Continues

II.SS-Pz.Korps and part of I.SS-Pz.Korps renewed their attacks in the course of the night of June 29/30, still with the aim of reversing the Allied breakthrough. On the Frundsberg right wing, SS-Pz.Gr.Rgt.21 attacked at 0130, succeeding shortly after in occupying Avenay and Vieux, where contact with III./SS-Pz.Gr.Rgt.26 was established. A few hours later, the Hitlerjugend attack was also launched: after preparatory fire from SS-Pz.Art.Rgt.12 and Werferregiment 83, the II./SS-Pz.Rgt.12 with elements of the III./26, attacked Hill 112 from the east and southeast. At the same time, elements of SS-Pz.Gr.Rgt.21 and II./SS-Pz.Rgt.10 attacked from the south and southwest. Except for a few tanks, the Allies had already withdrawn their armored units from the hill, still occupied by the 8th Rifle Battalion. The artillery and rockets had a devastating effect. The panzers were able to quickly take possession of the hill. Farther left, SS-Pz.Gr.Rgt.22 again attacked Gavrus. Artillery and mortar fire, as well as subsequent hand-to-hand combat, caused significant losses to the 2nd Argylls, who were forced to retire to Colleville.

In the early afternoon, the commander of II.SS-Pz.Korps, SS-Gruf. Bittrich, ordered the suspension of the attacks. And so, the third battle for Caen came to its conclusion. With overwhelming superiority, the Allies had failed to widen their breakthrough beyond the Orne and push on to the plain south of Caen. The Hitlerjugend can also take credit for this. During the battles for Hill 112 and in the Esquay area, SS-Ostubaf. Wünsche with his decimated Panzer-Regiment, SS-Aufkl.Abt.12 and the III./26, drove off all enemy attacks, as they had previously done at Fontenay and Rauray. His 30 panzers faced some 165 VIII Corps tanks over the course of June 28, and destroyed many. Finally, the action of I./26 led by SS-Stubaf. Krause, which prevented the capture of Carpiquet airfield by the 3rd Canadian Division, must be remembered. II./SS-Pz.Rgt.12 and III./26, together with the Frundsberg panzers and grenadiers, recaptured Hill 112, which became the focal point of the fighting in the following weeks. The division's total losses June 25–30 were 209 dead, 557 wounded, and 474 missing.

The Fourth Battle for Caen

After four weeks of fighting, Rommel recommended a strategic withdrawal to a new defensive line south of Caen, to pull German troops out of range of Allied naval artillery. However, when von Rundstedt made the proposal to the Führer on July 3, he was dismissed from his post and replaced by Generalfeldmarschall von Kluge.

General der Panzertruppen Heinrich Eberbach took over command of Panzergruppe West. Meanwhile, Montgomery had not abandoned his plan of wanting to destroy the SS divisions and besiege Caen. However, the Hitlerjugend stood like a rock among the German defenses, with its units positioned in a semicircle to the north of the city. The arrival of II.SS-Pz.Korps allowed Meyer's division to free itself from the responsibility of holding the western side of the defensive front and concentrating on the defense of Caen.

SS-Pz.Gr. Rgt.25, now commanded by SS-Ostubaf. Karl-Heinz Milius, defended the villages northwest of the city, while Mohnke's SS-Pz.Gr.Rgt.26 held the area to the west from the Carpiquet airfield. Meyer still had under his command the Leibstandarte *Kampfgruppe* which he deployed south of the airport. Wünsche's panzers held the eastern part of Hill 112. Frundsberg troops were firmly entrenched on the top of the same hill and on the nearby Hill 113, finally supported by s.SS-Pz.Abt.102. Tigers, Hohenstaufen was stationed

Ardenne Abbey, from left, SS-Ostubaf. Milius, SS-Stubaf. Meyer, SS-Ustuf. Reinecher, and SS-Ostuf. Meitzel. (Hubert Meyer collection)

along the northern bank of the Odon, in contact with the armored units of the army to the west. The German lines were anchored on a series of fortified villages defended by the *Panzergrenadieren*, while 8.8cm Flak pieces were positioned an open field between the villages, with the panzers even farther back, ready to counterattack on the heights to better control access to hills 112 and 113. The key to Caen, certainly the northern access, was the Carpiquet airfield which was heavily defended by Hitlerjugend units.

The Attack on Carpiquet

The first hint of trouble was on July 1 when units of the Leibstandarte were engaged in clashes along the Odon toward the west, as Allied troops looked to capture Verson and Fontaine-Etoupefour, threatening the western flank of Carpiquet's defensive ring. Lined up in the thrust against the airfield (Operation *Windsor*), Montgomery had at his disposal the 3rd Canadian Infantry Division, 8th Infantry Brigade, Royal Winnipeg Rifles, 10th Armoured Regiment, and special mine-clearing tanks and flamethrowers of the 79th Armoured Division, with the Queen's Own Rifles of Canada in reserve.

Enemy movement was detected as early as July 2, as reported in Panzergruppe West's daily report:

> The enemy is still reinforcing on the left wing of 12.SS-Pz.Div. The enemy is trying to determine the strength of our forces and the location of our positions with motorized patrols from the Marcelet area and south of it. These patrols were repelled by the fire of our artillery and mortars.

A Hitlerjugend Flak battery, Normandy, 1944.

Carpiquet airfield.

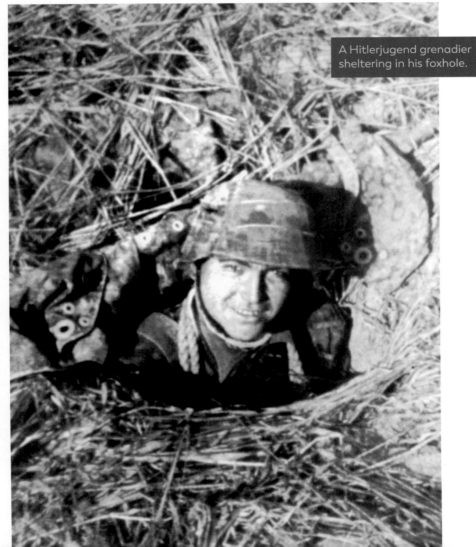

A Hitlerjugend grenadier sheltering in his foxhole.

On that same day, missing since June 26, SS-Ostuf. Alois Hartung returned to the German lines and reported that the Allies were preparing to attack, having noticed a sizable buildup of enemy units.

At dawn on July 4, preceded by a by a furious artillery, air force, and naval bombardment, the Allied attack began. The Queen's Own Rifles struck Carpiquet around 1100, attempting to capture the facilities on the eastern side of the airfield. But the Flak battery at the road fork to Saint-Germain-la-Blanche-Herbe stopped the tanks in their tracks. Artillery and mortar fire prevented the Royal Winnipeg Rifles from attacking the hangars on the southern side of the airfield. Canadian tanks were then sent forward, which got close to the hangars but were unable to dislodge the *Panzergrenadieren* and were forced to withdraw to the cover of a small wooded area west of the airfield.

In the afternoon, a fresh Allied attack was attempted, but once again was repulsed by the few panzers of 9.Pz.Kp. and some Panthers of 4.Pz.Kp., which arrived from Bretteville-sur-Odon. SS-Oscha Zugführer Richard Rudolf in his panzer destroyed six Shermans (and was later awarded the Knight's Cross). To break the impasse, RAF Typhoons intervened, but without appreciable results.

However, Carpiquet village was in Allied hands, threatening the entire airfield front. Hitlerjugend was entrusted with its recapture. Shortly after midnight, SS-Ostubaf. Wilhelm Weidenhaupt's III./SS-Pz.Gr.Rgt.1 regrouped with I./SS-Pz.Gr.Rgt.1 south of Route Nationale 13 and advanced on the village but came under enemy artillery fire. At the same time, wayward German artillery fire caused significant friendly-fire casualties. At dawn,

A Hitlerjugend troops and armor in a French village, 1944. (NARA)

In Profile:
SS-Brigadeführer und Generalmajor der Waffen-SS Wilhelm Mohnke

SS-Hstuf. Wilhelm Mohnke. (BDC)

Wilhelm Mohnke with the Knight's Cross.

Wilhelm Mohnke was born on March 15, 1911, in Lübeck. His father was a cabinetmaker. Mohnke held a degree in economics and was in senior business management before he enrolled in the NSDAP in September 1931. Showing much promise, he was posted to SS-Stabswache Berlin, and became a company commander in the unit's successor, SS-Sonderkommando Berlin. He was wounded during the invasion of Poland but recovered in time for the invasion of the Low Countries and the battle for France as a battalion commander in Leibstandarte SS Adolf Hitler (LSSAH). He was allegedly involved in the murder of 80 British and French prisoners of war. He was severely wounded in the leg in the Balkans campaign. Recovered, he joined the Hitlerjugend in June 1943 as CO 26th SS Panzergrenadier Regiment. He saw action during the Normandy campaign, again implicated in a massacre, the murder of 35 Canadian prisoners of war at Fontenay-le-Pesnel. He led the retreat of his *Kampfgruppe* with distinction during the retreat from the Falaise Pocket and was one of the few German commanders to offer any meaningful resistance along the Seine. On August 31, he took command of LSSAH which he commanded during the Ardennes offensive. It was on his watch that Peiper's troops murdered 68 American prisoners of war in the Malmedy Massacre. Mohnke was wounded yet again, this time on the Hungarian front, and withdrawn from active service. He commanded the Zitadelle sector during the battle of Berlin. He surrendered to the Red Army, eventually being released from imprisonment in 1955. He managed to avoid all charges of war crimes. He died, aged 90, on August 6, 2001 in Barsbüttel-Hamburg. He held the Iron Cross (1st and 2nd Class), Wound Badge, War Merit Cross, the German Cross in Gold, and the Knight's Cross of the Iron Cross.

with SS units reaching the railway line near Franqueville, the attack was called off in the face of staunch Allied resistance.

During the hiatus, the Germans took the opportunity to regroup. The 276.Inf.Div. relieved the Pz.-Lehr-Div. and the 16.Luftwaffe Feld-Division arrived in theater. On July 5, an order from the Führer's headquarters to withdraw the Hitlerjugend from the front in order to rest was ignored due to critical situation on the Caen front. The divisional CP meanwhile moved to the western area of Caen, to the old Abbaye aux Dames. As of July 7, the Hitlerjugend could boast 37 PzKpfw IVs and 24 Panthers on its inventory, deployed north and west of Buron, at Grunchy, northeast and west of Ardenne, west of Caen, on the eastern side of the Carpiquet airfield, and between Eterville and Bretteville-sur-Odon.

Operation *Charnwood*

I Corps engaged three infantry divisions for the offensive, the 3rd British, 3rd Canadian, and 59th Staffordshire, with two armored brigades, the 27th and 2nd Armoured Brigades, as well special demining and flamethrower tanks from the 79th Armoured Division. VIII Corps, for its part, would attack from the Odon bridgehead.

A ground and naval bombardment began in the afternoon of July 7; later that evening, 467 Halifax and Lancaster bombers dropped more than 2,500 tons of bombs on Caen, causing a firestorm which killed many French civilians. As soon as the bombers went home, VIII and I Corps artillery opened fire, targeting the communication lines in the south of the city.

At 0420 am on July 8, the infantry attack began, preceded by another artillery barrage. The 6th North Staffords and 2/6 South Staffords, supported by tanks, moved against La Bijude and Galmanche respectively. Bijude fell at 0730; however, a few pockets of grenadier resistance held out for two hours. Galmanche, defended by elements of II./25, under SS-Hstuf. Karl-Heinz Schrott, on the other hand, held out stubbornly, as reported in the 2/6 South Staffords' war diary:

> 4:20: start of the artillery preparation fire, with the troops that have left their departure positions. 4:30: the companies were repelled by an intense fire of machine guns and mortars. Heavy casualties, including many officers and non-commissioned officers. Some signs of disorientation between units. 7:30: the tanks report having reached their target, but no infantry can be seen, still halfway to their target.

The British 59th Infantry Division advanced on Epron and the 3rd Canadian Infantry Division on Buron, Gruchy, Château de Saint-Louis, and Authie, but ground to a stop under a barrage of artillery and Nebelwerfers and were forced to retreat.

At 0735, the 1/7 Warwicks, attacked Galmanche and Saint-Contest simultaneously. At Galmanche they were blocked by Willy Kändler's 5.Pz.Kp. panzers as bitter fighting erupted throughout the village. Once the Allied antitank guns were destroyed, the SS grenadiers dealt with the Allied tanks at close range with hand grenades and Panzerfausts. The commander of 6.Kp., SS-Hstuf. Anton Tiray, personally destroyed three Shermans with Panzerfausts but was killed while attempting to destroy a fourth.

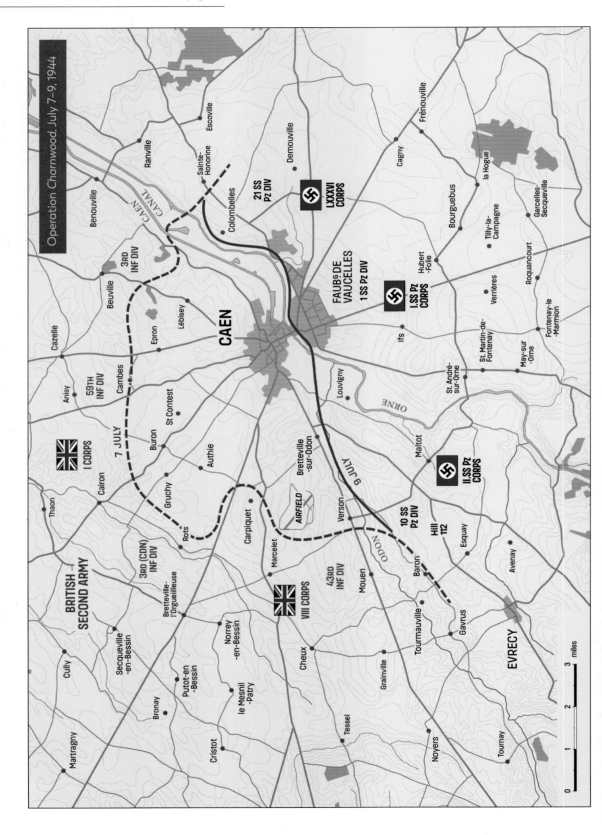

Operation Charnwood July 7-9, 1944

Hitlerjugend soldiers examine a destroyed Sherman, with entry holes near the tracks. (DWS)

At 0900, General Eberbach arrived at the Hitlerjugend CP, just as the first alarming reports began arriving: the Allies had broken through at Galmanche, Gruchy was lost, and Buron and Saint-Contest were under attack. Reinforcements were needed to stem the tide but there were none. The best Eberbach could do was to redeploy II./Pz.Rgt.22 to Caen.

At 1430 on June 8, the North Nova Scotia Highlanders broke through at Authie but came under fire from 3.Pz.Kp. led by *SS-Ustuf.* Bogensperger who destroyed several Shermans.

The survivors of III./25 surrounded at Buron continued to resist. CO Hauptmann Fritz Steger, still in radio contact with the regimental command at Ardenne, reported that most of his men were dead and that the Shermans were about to overwhelm them. He asked for reinforcements but all available panzers had been sent to Buron to attempt to break the encirclement and had failed. At the same time, Allied tanks attacked the SS-Pz.Gr.Rgt.25 CP but a desperate intervention by the division's panzers saw off the threat. The 2/5 Lancashire Fusiliers attack on I./25 was repulsed with heavy losses, forcing the British to withdraw the battalion from the front. By contrast, elements of the 3rd British Infantry Division had pushed to the outskirts of Caen, meeting little resistance, hampered only by the rubble. Other units, having bypassed I./25, threatened the crossings on the Orne. Waldmüller detached a platoon to protect his right flank, while an armored company arrived from the division as reinforcement.

South of the Orne

Hitler had ordered that Caen be defended at all costs and that no retreat would be contemplated. Only in the late evening, Sepp Dietrich was able to authorize a retreat of Hitlerjugend units on the southern bank of the Orne, thanks to a "gimmick" by his chief of staff, SS-Brigdf. Krämer, who said to Meyer: "If you are pushed back to the southern bank of the Orne, while fighting against superior enemy forces, this can in no way be judged as a retreat contrary to the orders received." Meyer immediately issued orders to his various units to withdraw to Caen during the night. The artillery and mortars were to cross to the southern bank of the Orne to secure, and prepare to blow, the bridges. His CP would move south of Caen to Vaucelles.

At 1915 on July 9, Rommel authorized the general withdrawal of the Hitlerjugend despite the Führer's orders. At the same time, the Canadian Scottish broke through at Cussy: 1.Flak.Batterie, commanded by SS-Hstuf. Ritzel, fought to the last man. falling at their guns. The Queen's Rifles and the Regina Rifles advanced on Ardenne under heavy fire, sustaining significant casualties. I Corps motorized recon units advanced along Route Nationale 13 from Bayeux, but were blocked by minefields and German infantry fire in front of Caen.

Waldmüller's I./25 continued to resist the continuous Allied assaults on his position as reported by the commander of the 1.Kompanie, engaged on the battalion's right flank, Oberleutnant F.

A Hitlerjugend antitank gun and a Panther destroyed during the fighting northwest of Caen. A dead gunner lies beside his gun.

A dazed and wounded Hitlerjugend grenadier surrenders. (NARA)

After a new round of artillery preparatory fire, the enemy attacked again and this time with flamethrowing tanks. This initially caused some panic, however the company remained steadfast in its positions. And this despite most of the young grenadiers having their first experience on the front line under enemy fire. After the destruction of the first enemy tank with antitank weapons, morale was completely raised. This first success gave courage and other tanks were destroyed in the same way. The attack was then repulsed.

The I./25 retreat was finally possible, only because the first platoon of 1.Kompanie was able to prevent another enemy breakthrough on the right flank. SS-Ostuf. Schümann, commander of 1./25, and many of his men were killed during the bitter fighting. The few survivors continued to fight desperately for another two days. Even the survivors of 7.Kompanie managed to retreat from Galmanche, after having fought superior enemy forces and repelled numerous assaults, arriving in Caen during the night.

The Allies had meanwhile achieved most of their objectives although pockets of resistance held out west of Epron and Buron into the night. In the central sector, Mâlon, Couvre-Chef, La Folie, Bitot, part of Galmanche, and Ardenne were abandoned by the Germans; but the Allies had failed to establish a bridgehead on the Orne near Caen.

During the night and at first light of July 9, the survivors of SS-Pz.Gr.Rgt.25 marched through the ruins of Caen, crossing the only bridge still intact over the Orne, to settle into new defensive positions. Divisional command was transferred to Garcelles. At around 0700, Allied troops arrived at Couvre-Chef, while Bitot and La Folie fell that afternoon. Around noon, the vanguard of the 3rd British Division entered Caen, encountering little resistance.

The Divisionbegleitkompanie was attacked by superior Allied forces around 1000 and forced to retreat to Caen, continuing to fight a rearguard action all the way. III./26, under attack by the Canadians, withdrew to the city and the bridge over the Orne. SS-Stubaf. Olboeter was the last to cross the bridge, and ordered the SS engineers to blow it.

Operations *Jupiter* and *Greenline*

Having occupied northern Caen, Montgomery continued to attack on July 10, as part of a new operation, *Jupiter*, to establish bridgeheads on the Orne. In particular, the 43rd Wessex Division was ordered to drive the Germans off Hill 112 and open the way to the Orne for the 4th Armoured Brigade.

Operation *Jupiter* began with the usual artillery barrage, followed by two infantry brigades supported by Churchill heavy tanks attacking Hill 112 and the village of Maltot, positioned on its northern side. The British attempted to cover their attack with a smokescreen

Hitlerjugend grenadiers in action among the ruins of Caen.

A Hitlerjugend halftrack on the march. (NARA)

A I./SS-Pz.Art.Rgt.12 self-propelled gun. (NARA)

A Hitlerjugend Panther in the ruins of Caen.

which only obscured the view of their artillery observers. The *Panzergrenadieren* clashed with waves of British infantry, while 8.8cm guns stalled an entire regiment of Churchill tanks. Another tank formation, consisting of 25 Churchills, that was about to take the summit of Hill 112, was decimated by the Frundsberg armored battalion that had deployed from its reserve position. The British 17-pounder antitank guns managed to damage several Tigers, but the German defenses on the northern side of the hill held: as many as 43 Allied tanks were destroyed.

Simultaneous with the attack on Hill 112, the 130th Brigade attacked Maltot: three infantry regiments backed by Churchill tanks advanced in the open to achieve their objectives on the northern bank of the Orne. After making good progress, the British brigade soon found itself under German fire from three sides: SS-Pz.Abt.102 Tigers opened fired on the British left flank, Hitlerjugend Panthers and PzKpfw IVs opened fire head-on, and the Leibstandarte *Kampfgruppe* opned up from the right. Within minutes, the British lost almost all their tanks. SS-Ustuf. Willi Kändler, again in the thick of the action, was deployed along the Louvigny–Maltot road and destroyed at least seven enemy tanks, while the number of tanks destroyed by the rest of the platoon is unknown. At the same time, infantrymen of the Hampshire and Dorset Regiments broke into Maltot. SS-Brigdf. Harmel's Frundsberg recon battalion, with supporting fire from the Tigers, destroyed all the Dorsets' antitank guns, forcing the British to withdraw.

Meanwhile, on Hill 112, Duke of Cornwall infantry launched an attack, reaching the summit, threatening to wrest the key position from the Germans. Dietrich and Bittrich once again had to commit their last reserves. The Hohenstaufen, now commanded by SS-Staf.

Heinz Harmel, in the center with the Knight's Cross, aboard his command vehicle. (MNZS)

Sylvester Stadler, was ordered to retake the hill. During the night, SS units moved on the hill, waiting for artillery fire support fire. The congested streets delayed the attack considerably and when it was launched, the *Panzergrenadieren* found themselves under heavy artillery fire. At dawn, the SS had to withdraw to avoid further losses.

In the early afternoon, the Duke of Cornwall infantry regiment was literally torn to pieces by German fire, while the Hohenstaufen assault guns launched a new attack which left at least 250 British dead and wounded, including the regiment's CO, on top of the hill. The Germans thus regained control of the hill which remained in their hands for the rest of the month.

On July 15, Montgomery launched Operation *Greenline*, to attempt once again to expand the British front in the Odon valley and at the same time keep II.SS-Pz.Korps engaged, while armored forces massed for an offensive east of Caen. An Allied breakthrough at Noyers immediately forced Bittrich to send the Hohenstaufen to close the breach on July 16: 20 panzers were scraped together and deployed from Hill 113 in the direction of the Odon. The SS tanks clashed with a British armored brigade and destroyed 48 Shermans and captured a dozen, while the Germans lost five panzers.

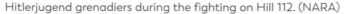

Hitlerjugend grenadiers during the fighting on Hill 112. (NARA)

Hitlerjugend grenadiers in Normandy. (NARA)

| Epilogue

After six weeks of attritional warfare, from the beaches of Normandy to the ruins of the city of Caen, the Hitlerjugend was placed in reserve. It had been a desperate defense at Caen, with too few resources and too few troops, coupled with poor strategic leadership—Hitler's interference—that had allowed the British, Canadian and Polish forces to start breaking through into Caen.

That General Montgomery was planning yet another massive offensive was obvious: from the Bourguébus Heights, the Germans enjoyed a commanding view of the Caen area, so it was almost impossible for the Allies to mask their preparations. For the forthcoming assault, Montgomery would field the three armored divisions of the VIII Corps, 11th, Guards, and 7th Armoured, with 877 tanks in total, supported by 10,000 infantry and 8,000 other vehicles, with formidable artillery and aviation fire support, with 712 guns, 942 RAF bombers, and 571 USAAF bombers.

To stem the forthcoming Allied offensive, the two SS divisions, Hitlerjugend and Leibstandarte, as well as some Luftwaffe and Heer panzer units, could assemble around 200 tanks, 50 assault guns, 36 7.5cm antitank guns, 72 8.8cm Flak guns, 194 artillery pieces, and

A British rifleman in Caen, completely destroyed by the Allied bombings, which caused significant casualties among the civilian population. (Imperial War Museum)

Knight's Cross recipients, from left, Mohnke, Wünsche, Dietrich, Meyer, and Prinz.

17 Nebelwerfer batteries. Vastly outnumbered, the Waffen-SS divisions would be squeezed out of Caen and into the *Kessel*, the cauldron, of the Falaise Pocket. Moments of tactical and individual brilliance à la Michael Wittman would be desperately required if the SS divisions were to stave off total annihilation.

| Bibliography

Public Archives

Bundesmilitär-Archiv, Freiburg, Germany
Deutsche Dienststelle (WASt)
Vojensky Historicky Archiv (Military History Archives, Prague, Czech Republic)
Washington, D.C. National Archives & Records Administration (NARA)

Periodicals & Documentaries

Armes Militaria Magazine: various issues
Das Schwarze Korps magazine: various issues
Der Freiwillige magazine: various issues
Die Deutsche Wochenschau films
Ritterkreuz magazine, bi-monthly dedicated to Waffen-SS formations: various issues
Siegrunen, magazine, a periodical published by Richard Landwehr: various issues
Signal magazine: various editions and issues

Books

Bernage, Georges & Meyer, H., *12 SS-Panzer Division Hitlerjugend* (Bayeux: Editions Heimdal, 1991)
Bernage, Georges, *The Panzers and the Battles of Normandy* (Bayeux: Editions Heimdal, 2009)

A Panther tank advances.

Bishop, Chris, *Waffen-SS Divisions 1939–45* (London: Amber Books, 2007)

Butler, Rupert, *SS-Hitlerjugend: The History of the Twelfth SS Division 1943–45* (Staplehurst: Spellmount, 2015)

Cockle, Tom & Volstad, Ronald, *Hitler Youth and the 12.SS-Panzer-Division Hitlerjugend 1933–1945* (Hong Kong: Concord Publications Company, 2004)

Duprat, François, *Les campagnes de la Waffen SS* (Paris: Les Sept Couleurs, 1973)

Jeanne, F., *Caen Juillet 1944: la bataille finale* (Bayeux: Editions Heimdal, 2010)

Kompanie-Kameradschaft, *Die 3.Kompanie SS-Panzer-Regiment 12, 12.SS-Panzerdivision "Hitlerjugend,"* private publication.

Kraetschmer, Ernst-Günther, *Die Ritterkreuztraeger der Waffen-SS* (Preussisch Oldendorf: K.W. Schütz, 1982)

Landemer, Henri, *La Waffen SS* (Paris: Balland, 1972)

Lewis, Brenda Ralph, *The Hitlerjugend in War and Peace 1933–1945* (St. Paul: MBI Publishing Company, 2000)

Lumsden, Robin, *La vera storia delle SS* (Rome: Newton & Compton Editori, 2017)

Luther, Craig, *Blood and Honor: The History of the 12th SS Panzer Division Hitlerjugend* (R. James Bender Publishing, 2012)

Maier, Georg, *Drama zwischen Budapest und Wien. Der Endkampf der 6. Panzerarmee 1945* (Trier: Munin-Verlag, 1985)

Meyer, Hubert, *Kriegsgeschichte der 12.SS-Panzer-Division "Hitlerjugend"* (Trier: Munin Verlag GmbH, 1998)

Meyer, Kurt, *Grenadiers* (Mechanicsburg: Stackpole Books, 2005)

Natkiel, Richard & Young, Peter, *Atlante della Seconda guerra mondiale* (Milano: Mondadori editore, 1958)

Neulen, Hans Werner, *An deutscher Seite, Internationale Freiwillige von Wehrmacht und Waffen SS* (Stuttgart: Universitas, 1985)

Reynolds, Michael, *Steel Inferno, 1st SS Panzer Korps in Normandy* (New York: Dell Publishing, 1998)

Stein, George H., *The Waffen-SS: Hitler's Elite Guard at War 1939–1945* (Ithaca: Cornell University Press, 1944)

Tessin, Georg, *Verbande und truppen der deutschen Wermacht und Waffen-SS,* (Osnabrück: Biblio Verlag, 1965)

Walther, Herbert, *The 12th SS Panzer Division* (Atglen: Schiffer Publishing, 1989)

Williamson, Gordon, *Storia Illustrata delle SS* (Rome: Newton & Compton editori)

Websites

www.axishistory.com

www.corazzati.it

www.feldgrau.com

www.lexikon-der-wehrmacht.de

www.maxafiero.it

www.okh.it

| Index

Other Titles in the Casemate Illustrated Series:

12TH SS PANZER DIVISION HITLERJUGEND
FROM OPERATION *GOODWOOD* TO APRIL 1945
by Massimiliano Afiero

Packed with photographs, maps and profiles, this Casemate Illustrated title follows the actions of the infamous 12th SS Panzer Division 'Hitlerjugend' throughout its existence.

COMING OUT 2023 | 9781636243146

GERMAN ARMOR IN NORMANDY
by Yves Buffetaut

This volume looks at the German armored forces in Normandy in 1944, focusing on the organization of the 10 Panzer divisions that fought in Normandy, the vehicles they relied on and the battles they fought in.

OUT NOW | 9781612006437

THE WAFFEN-SS IN NORMANDY
by Yves Buffetaut

This volume follows how the Waffen-SS fared in Normandy during June 1944 and whether they deserved their reputation of being the ultimate fighting soldiers.

OUT NOW | 9781612006055

THE 3RD SS PANZER REGIMENT
by Pierre Tiquet

A highly illustrated account of SS-Panzer Regiment Totenkopf from 1943 to 1945, based on veteran memoirs.

OUT NOW | 9781612007311

THE 2ND SS PANZER DIVISION DAS REICH
by Yves Buffetaut

A fully illustrated history of the 2nd SS-Panzer 'Das Reich' Division, from their pre-war formation, through the Blitzkrieg campaigns and Barbarossa to Normandy and their final surrender in May 1945.

OUT NOW | 9781612005256